THY
WORD
HAVE I HID
IN MINE
HEART

THY
WORD
HAVE I HID
IN MINE
HEART

VERNON GILBERT

THY WORD HAVE I HID IN MINE HEART

Scripture quotations marked KJV are from the Holy Bible, King James Version (Authorized Version). First published in 1611. Quoted from the KJV Classic Reference Bible, Copyright © 1983 by The Zondervan Corporation.

iUniverse books may be ordered through booksellers or by contacting:

iUniverse
1663 Liberty Drive
Bloomington, IN 47403
www.iuniverse.com
1-800-Authors (1-800-288-4677)

ISBN: 978-1-4917-8616-1 (sc)
ISBN: 978-1-4917-8617-8 (e)

Library of Congress Control Number: 2015921204

Print information available on the last page.

iUniverse rev. date: 02/11/2016

DEDICATION

This book is dedicated to Shirley Ruth Higginbotham Gilbert, my dear wife of some sixty-two years as of this printing. That time span is also four generations because Shirley is the mother of our four children, and by extension, our twenty-five grandchildren and almost that many great-grandchildren. She not only raised our four precious children, but has been a full partner in our business since its inception. In the early years of the business she tirelessly worked in all departments, some weeks seeing her put in over a hundred hours duty. In those years her dining table was frequently covered with construction projects, building alarm system components and equipment. Much of the time she was helping with these projects herself, along with her many other varied responsibilities. She helped operate the armored car service, and holstered a sidearm to meet the insurance company's requirement. Training for this need, we discovered Shirley has a natural gift in shooting a handgun – using either hand, since she is ambidextrous. Shirley has used her high school skills and a short bookkeeping course to allow her to serve as our only accountant, even filing tax forms in our early years. She served on the Board of Directors for many years until she and I stepped down recently to make room for the younger people in the company. When I got the writing bug a few years ago, Shirley was, as always, most supportive of my efforts and has helped in every way imaginable attending to the many varied responsibilities of producing books. She was able to obtain the needed 501 (c) (3) classification for our charitable foundation and serves on that board. Shirley is co-authoring a children's book with me, and I think she plans to hide the word processor from me to help me find something else to fill my golden years. She is a very self-effacing person who never seeks the limelight nor brags on herself. That's what husbands are for after all.

ACKNOWLEDGEMENTS

Most of the message in this book is the direct results of the many people entrusted by God to produce the most import and enduring book, His Holy Bible. To accurately bring this to our English language, from the original tongues, we have the King James translators to thank. The poor commentary by me had to be proof read, mostly by Mona and Shirley to make it readable. If it has typos or errors contained they are my responsibility because I read the final galleys as my fourth trek through it all. The helpful people at iUniverse worked very well meeting and surpassing our expectations. Randy, again took the pages of text and put them in proper order for submission to the publishers. He did the necessary work to get it in the form they required. Thanks to the combined efforts of these and other people, Shirley and I have a unique opportunity to share our joy in memorizing Scripture with many people we will never have a chance to meet this side of Jordan. We are indebted to everyone who buys this book and shares its message with others. We hope and pray the royalty stream from the sales will help sustain the worthwhile efforts of the foundation in years to come, perhaps until the return of the Lord Jesus to rule in perfect peace.

THY WORD HAVE I HID IN MINE HEART ...

This title is the opening half of *Psalms 119:11,* as rendered in the King James version of the Bible. It concludes with *...,that I might not sin against Thee.* This passage is a promise from David to hold God's message in his innermost being, so he will not wander off the narrow way of God, into the broad bramble paths of Satan. In the days of King David, there were no books as we know them today, and the papyrus used for writing scrolls was bulky and expensive. Most of the people were illiterate anyway, and most information was interchanged orally-by word of mouth. Each one of us has a built-in scratch pad called our memory. Things stored in a healthy brain can be retained for a lifetime, to be retrieved whenever we want to recall events, scenes, words, or whatever. A grandmother asked a very young grandson how he had recalled an earlier event, and he proudly replied that he had a "rememberer." Well Jeffry, thank the Lord we all have a rememberer.

Shirley memorized lots of things in her early childhood and teens. She can easily recall the lyrics of songs that were popular when she was in high school. She committed some verses of the Bible, as a Sunday school attendee, to memory which she can recite today. She encouraged me for years, to do likewise. My answer was that since Gutenberg invented the press, we now have Bibles to hold those Scriptures for us. I remember her reply that the day might come when we don't have Bibles as readily available as we currently have. I thought that was worrying about something that would <u>never</u> happen in this country. Recently, I see things which change my perspective. Military chaplains ordered to remove Bibles from their desktops, Bibles prohibited from hospital rooms, hotel and motel rooms, and our school properties. Our ungodly leadership people practicing political correctness are fine with the school kids having pornography,

Korans, and witchcraft books, but a New Testament in one's locker can get a kid in trouble! Who would have thought it?

Several years ago, Shirley and I were privileged to attend a gathering of church people at a large Baptist church in the Houston area. She attended an "Experiencing God" seminar, and I enrolled in their "Master Life" program. We both learned some great truths that have been useful ever since. One of the objects of the course I was in, was to memorize a Scripture passage each night and be able to recite it for the group the next day. The first such passage assigned was *Luke 9:23,* and we were using a Disciples edition of the NIV. I sort of dragged my feet, but got with the program when I saw how the rest of the class of fourteen preachers and missionaries were accepting the assignment. That Scripture in fact, teaches the importance of attending to our duties in a responsible, timely manner. It says in the KJV *And He said to them all, If any man will come after me, let him deny himself, and take up his cross daily, and follow me.* Taking that bit of Scripture to heart, I enjoyed the unique opportunity offered, by applying myself and learning a lot of truth from the lady instructor and my fellow students.

Shirley, being a good helpmate, memorized the passage in the King James wording, as well as the other Scriptures in my program. Likewise, we studied the entire *Experiencing God* workbook and memorized several of the drills in it, such as the seven realities, four steps and four ways. Memorization is just one of the things she surpasses my best efforts in. I stuffed down my pride enough to get enthusiastic concerning memory verse practice. In the next several years, we often spent time practicing with one reciting and the other following the printed text. Gary, and Randy later, used a computer app to print the passages we had selected, and we carried those with us when we traveled. In recent years, I still recite favorite Scripture to myself, whenever circumstances require my waiting on people or events. We haven't pursued the memory work recently as we did, but we both want to get back into it. At the apex of our memory verse recitation, Shirley could go for an hour and forty-five minutes with 99% accuracy!

Just as we are not to become prideful of other gifts given to us by God, likewise we must not forget where the "rememberers" we have came from. A couple of somewhat humorous events come to mind, as I put this in the word processor, which I can share with the reader. Once, we were visiting my elderly Aunt Bessie in Fort Worth, and we all went to her church for Sunday morning services. I went to the senior men's Sunday school class, where some 15-20 gentlemen were gathered. The teacher arrived just in time to call the class to order, and he directed one of them to give me a quarterly class book. This was in a large, older, Southern Baptist church, and they had all the Scripture in NIV or some other new age rendition and in the King James as well. Scanning the lesson as the others were discussing "them cowboys" and such, I saw the lesson was centered on *Esther 4:14*, one of our memory verses. When the teacher asked if anyone had committed the assigned memory verse, and no one responded, the teacher started to commence, and I gingerly raised my hand. I believe to this day, the Holy Spirit gave me the ability to deliver the entire forty-eight words of that Scripture, in one smoothly voiced oratory. The teacher, visibly taken aback, managed to stammer "Thank you – sir," and the others looked like they wondered who let this turkey into our church. After the class was over, not one of those men visited with me during the time before the preaching service began, nor after the services.

The other time familiarity with a Scripture resulted in a humorous incident, was when we were attending the trade days event in Canton, Texas. Inside one of the larger tent areas, was a vendor who had a variety of handmade decorative items displayed for sale. One such thing was a section of a log slice, with Scripture burned into the surface, before the artist finished it with varnish. One of these larger works had the title, *Psalm 1 from the KJV.* Admiring the beautiful wood grain and handiwork, I noted the words only contained the first three verses of chapter one, omitting the closing three. Displayed was: *V1-Blessed is the man that walketh not in the counsel of the ungodly, nor standeth in the way of sinners, nor sitteth in the seat of the scornful. V2-But his delight is in the law of the LORD; and in His law doth he meditate day and night. V3- And he shall be like a tree planted by the rivers of water, that bringeth forth his fruit in his season; his leaf also shall not wither; and whatsoever he doeth shall prosper.* The concluding verses, omitted here, say: *V4 – The ungodly are not so: but are like the chaff which the wind driveth away. V5 – Therefore the ungodly shall not stand in the judgment, nor sinners in the congregation of the righteous. V6 – For the LORD knoweth the way of the righteous: but the way of the ungodly shall perish.* The vendor saw me admiring his wares and came over to listen to me discussing the beautiful red cedar slab and the craftsmanship. When I said it really should be identified as a portion of the first chapter, he quickly assured me that was the complete Scripture. When I demurred, he became somewhat agitated and hurried out to his van to get his Bible. He returned somewhat more slowly and considerably subdued to agree he had been wrong. At lunch I related this all to Shirley, and at my suggestion, she visited the location that afternoon. When the man saw her looking at this piece he came over to talk to her. When she said that wasn't all of Psalm1, Mr. businessman rejoined with, "Yes, you're correct, but that is all of the good part."

Of much more importance than these two lighthearted incidents, are the numerous times when knowledge of Scripture can assist in allowing one to share God's Word and wisdom with others who are searching for answers to everyday problems. Among believers who are discussing what to do about a matter, a short "Thus saith the Lord," ends the discussion with a clear path to pursue. I think Jesus was accurately quoting Old Testament Scripture when His listeners marveled at His teaching as being from one with authority (Matthew 7:29 and Mark 1:22). We should thank the Lord every day for His wisdom and guidance contained in the Bible, for our use in choosing the strait gate path in our lives.

Back to my earlier reference to quoting well-known passages while waiting on people or events. ... I have had a problem with impatience all my life. Someone taking a lot of time to do something they should have done earlier, or someone running late for the umpteenth time has often led to my overreacting; and my making things worse for them and myself. I have learned to relax and recall as many of my favorite memory verses as the delay requires, repeating if needed. This simple drill serves me very well, makes the delay time really fly by, and has me in a good mood when the traffic gets moving, or "The doctor will see you now," is finally announced. Some good ones for this are The Lord's Prayer at Matthew 6:9-13 and Mark 11:2-4, Psalm 1, and 23 and 27:1, Micah 6:8, and 2 Chronicles 7:14. Two of our very best resources in dealing with the evil, wicked world we live in are fervent prayer and close familiarity with God's Maintenance Manual for mankind, His Holy Bible.

Genesis 1:1-5

1 *In the beginning God created the heaven and the earth.*

2 *And the earth was without form, and void; and darkness was upon the face of the deep. And the Spirit of God moved upon the face of the waters.*

3 *And God said, let there be light: and there was light.*

4 *And God saw the light, that it was good: and God divided the light from the darkness.*

5 *And God called the light Day, and the darkness He called Night. And the evening and the morning were the first day.*

This somewhat bare bones recital establishes for believers how Creation occurred and who was/is responsible for it all. Darwin and many others have offered their theories as to how the universe and its inhabitants came about. Man always invents in his evil mind different schemes to ignore the God of Creation and dismiss Him and send Him to the back of the bus. Throughout history, man has worshiped many, many different gods. The world's religions of this present time are no different. The fact stands however, that the Genesis account is the <u>only</u> place where anyone makes a credible claim for Creation. Here we have God's unmitigated statement that He did it. Later, in the Gospel of John we see the exact personage of the Holy Trinity, who is credited in Scripture as the Creator of all things.

The second verse shows that the earth was first created *without form* and in total darkness when *the Spirit of God moved upon the face of the waters.* This identifies the third member of the Trinity as being involved also. That is to my thinking, the same Spirit of God who was in the form of a dove, seen alighting at Jesus' baptism in the river Jordan, by John the Baptist. The same Holy Spirit who came at Pentecost as promised by Jesus. The same Holy Spirit who indwells every believer as our great Comforter today.

The third verse recounts the act of giving light to the world by our Creator. This is reminiscent of the mention in the first chapter of John's Gospel, identifying Jesus Christ as the *light of men* which shined in darkness without man's comprehension. After this reference to light and darkness here, the two conditions are mentioned many other times in the Bible. Light is usually associated with good and truth, while darkness is equated with evil and sinfulness.

In the fourth verse, we indeed see light identified as a good thing by God, and He divided it from the darkness. This can be thought of as an early indication that the two don't lend themselves to admixture. Today, a follower of Christ cannot be happy living in the light of His Gospel, while dabbling in the darkness of sin – evil – corruption. A good reference point addressing this can be seen in the Gospel of John at 3:19-21, which we plan to discuss when we cover that area of memory verses.

Verse five announces that God gave the names of day and night, setting the night before the day, even as modern Jews do today. It is also interesting to notice in this verse, the two divisions of time are capitalized in the Bible where they are first mentioned. Elsewhere in God's Word they are not so treated. If one is so impressed with Darwin's theory or some other unlikely hypothesis as to create a question in their mind regarding the truth, they should pray for the wisdom and faith to accept the truth from the One who was there and <u>knows.</u>

We should all be thankful to the Lord for daily truths from Him – the truths which He told us would make us free. God told us the facts from His firsthand knowledge, and He will not amend His report, for He does not change (Malachi 3:6). He is the same ... *same yesterday, and today, and forever* (Hebrews 13:8.) Whenever someone asks us what we think of the "big bang" theory or some such mental trash, we can use a small part of a good memory verse and reply, "In the beginning God created the heaven and the earth." We can aver this with conviction, because it is a direct quote from the God of all Creation – the <u>only God of all Creation.</u>

Genesis 1:27 – *So God created man in His own image, in the image of God created He him; male and female Created He them.*

Genesis *2:7 – And the LORD God formed man of the dust of the ground, and breathed into his nostrils the breath of life; and man became a living soul.*

Thank our Creator for these two simple, easy to comprehend verses. Nothing about an ape man nor evolving over a period of "millions and millions of years." No unexplainable big bang or lightning bolt to energize some ooze in a prehistoric swamp. No embarrassing questions of whence came the ape, the swamp, ooze, nor lightning bolt. When people discuss these deep questions, we can offer the only answer given by the One who has never told a single lie (Numbers 23:19 – Titus 1:2 – Hebrews 6:18). Incidentally, nearby these passages is the obvious answer to the question of which came first, the chicken or the egg? Mentioned is a list of animals He created, but no mention of any eggs.

Since we are told at John 4:24, that God is spirit, and the statement here that He created us in His image, it seems as if we resemble our Maker in our spirit rather than physically. Since we are told He made man and woman you might think He meant for us to have different, if similar roles in His grand scheme. Since we were created from dirt – *dust of the ground* – we should take a hint from the Scripture as to what our actual importance on earth is. Paul further expounds on this subject matter of man's prideful self-evaluation in Romans 12: 3, which we plan to cover when we get there. It is amazing how the Bible agrees in the various books written thousands of years apart by diverse writers who, for the most part, never knew one another. Even in the somewhat limited scope of the Scriptures we are addressing in this book, there are many verses that agree with and expound on one another while never differing in their message. Even a cursory inspection of the Koran, Book of Mormon, and other so called holy books will reveal inconsistencies and/or revisions and rewrites. The only exception in Bible versions is where man has re-written God's Holy Word to fit man's agenda in many of the hundreds of new age printings dreamed up since the old, trusted King James Version of 1604. When evil man decides to make acts that God refers to as abominations acceptable and endeavors to give such sin a thin patina of respectability, they print a new improved "bible" to fool everybody. Such inane foolishness is on a par with the weatherman on television lying about the freezing weather, expecting it to be balmy because he wants to go to the seashore to work on his tan.

Genesis 3:14-15 – *And the LORD God said unto the serpent, Because thou hast done this, thou art cursed above all cattle, and above every beast of the field; upon thy belly shalt thou go, and dust shalt thee eat all the days of thy life: and I will put enmity between thee and the woman, and between thy seed and her seed; it shall bruise thy head, and thou shall bruise his heel.*

Do you like snakes? - I don't, and reading this Scripture suggests we aren't expected to, by our Creator. Of course, reading this in context shows God was admonishing the serpent (Satan) for leading Eve to disobey God. The enmity God established between man and snakes is pretty universal. Sad to say however, our natural-born sin nature tends to lead us to delight in Satan's web of sinful lies today, just as Adam and Eve did in partaking of the fruit God had forbidden them to eat. These verses agree with many other messages throughout the Bible, that establish the accuracy of the core content showing that man is sinful in nature and is quite powerless to extract himself from the morass of worldly sin. This truth is at loggerheads with the politically correct stance of secular humanism, teaching that man is basically good by nature, requiring only more education and support from the government to evolve to his highest calling. It seems to me that we can understand from these words of wisdom that the rattlesnake and the cobra represent in physical nature the same deadly consequences as the devil does in the spiritual realm. Man runs the same danger to himself in playing with a coral snake as he does in playing with Satan's luring enticements. There is one very important difference however, in that the snake's poison <u>can</u> end our life here on earth, while the devil's poison always <u>does</u> lead to eternal separation from the Lord ..., **FOREVER!**

Genesis 6:5-8 – *And God saw that the wickedness of man was great in the earth, and that every imagination of the thoughts of his heart was only evil continually. 6 And it repented the LORD that He had made man on the earth, and it grieved Him at His heart. 7 And the LORD said, I will destroy man whom I have created from the face of the earth; both man, and beast, and the creeping thing, and the fowls of the air; for*

*it repenteth me that I have made them. 8 But Noah found grace in the
eyes of the Lord.*

That sounds pretty drastic to our tender ears. What had these
neighbors of Noah been doing to cause their Creator to decide on
such terrible retribution? The supporting passages tell that wickedness
was rampant and that the Lord rued the fact that He ever made
them. God was displeased in the evil of His Creation. We sometimes
wonder how ungodly, evil, and corrupt God will allow our country to
become before He exercises judgment on us. With all that God saw
the people doing, it mentions in the Bible that men were marrying
women and carrying on in their own manners as pleased themselves.
Today we see our own people killing a million babies each year,
because the little ones would cramp the selfish people's style. We are
legalizing same sex "marriages" while banning the Bible and cross
of Jesus in all public life. A better question of when God will say
"enough" is ask why He hasn't already done so. Our most loving
Creator extended compassion to Noah and his family, just as He did
to Lot and his. Neither of these men was perfect, of course, nor does
He demand perfection in us today. To get a sound feeling of His
requirements, go to Micah 6:8. The list is short; we plan to expand
on it in more detail when we have studied the memory verses between
here and there.

Genesis 7:23-24 – *And every living substance was destroyed which was
upon the face of the ground, both man, and cattle, and the creeping
things, and the fowl of the heaven; and they were destroyed from the
earth: and Noah only remained alive, and they that were with him in the
ark. 24 – And the waters prevailed upon the earth an hundred and fifty
days.*

And the Koran of Islam tells the reader that the Flood of Noah
was just a local weather thing! Reading this biblical account shows
us that God not only enacted a massive retribution on the evil of
Noah's time, but He also went to great pains to leave a record filled
with minute details. One message that requires little imagination
for anyone raised on a farm with animals, is that God preserves His
people, but they can still expect some valleys in their lives. Can you
imagine the smell in that ark with all of those animals shut up for five

months? The ventilation system was apparently rather restricted. We aren't told if there was a sun deck, but if there was, can you think how popular it would have been after the first week or so?

Genesis 9:13-16 – *I do set my bow in the cloud, and it shall be for a token of a covenant between me and the earth. 14 – And it shall come to pass, when I bring a cloud over the earth, that the bow shall be seen in the cloud: 15 – And I will remember my covenant, which is between me and you and every living creature of all flesh; and the waters shall no more become a flood to destroy all flesh. 6 – And the bow shall be in the cloud; and I will look upon it, that I may remember the everlasting covenant between God and every living creature of all flesh that is upon the earth.*

That bow is understood as being the rainbow we are all familiar with, usually seen after a rain has watered our plants and soaked some of us. This covenant was established between our Maker and us thousands of years before we read and memorize it. After enjoying this breathtakingly magnificent display for over fourscore years, it still impresses me with its natural beauty. A few times during those years we have observed a rain <u>circle</u> when flying in a small airplane a mile or so above the surface. When this happens, if you have good eyesight and look carefully, you can see the shadow image of the aircraft in the exact center of that colorful ring of reflected, refracted sunlight.

Genesis 15:5-7,18 – *And He brought him forth abroad, and said, look now toward heaven, and tell the stars, if thou be able to number them: and He said unto him, so shall thy seed be. 6 – And he believed in the LORD; and He counted it to him for righteousness. 7 – And He said unto him, I am the LORD that brought thee out of Ur of the Chaldees, to give thee this land to inherit it. 18 – In the same day the LORD made a covenant with Abram, saying, unto thy seed have I given this land, from the river of Egypt unto the great river, the river Euphrates:*

This is an account of God dealing with Abraham, before God changed his name from Abram. They are discussing the homeland of the descendants of Abraham. Of course, God knew already who the seed (descendants) of Abraham were going to be. It seems He was speaking of the Jews from Abraham through his wife Sarah, <u>and</u> the

Arabs through her handmaid Hagar. Well, the Jews reunited after thousands of years of being kicked around all over the world, when the nation of Israel was established in 1948. They now occupy only a small sliver of God's promise to Abraham. They live in the only pleasant part of the promised land, surrounded by the descendants of Hagar on three sides with the Mediterranean Sea on the fourth. The descendants of Hagar's son with Abraham are dedicated to pushing the Jews into that sea. Peek over to the sixteenth chapter of Genesis, and you can see that the Angel of God told Hagar that her descendants will be wild men with their hand against everyone. And so it is even today; they fight among themselves in endless wars and their religion directs them to be converting by force, or subjugating, or killing all Jews and Christians.

Genesis 28:12-15 – *And he dreamed, and behold a ladder set up on the earth, and the top of it reached to heaven: and behold the angels of God ascending and descending on it. 13 – And, behold, the LORD stood above it, and said, I am the LORD God of Abraham thy father, and the God of Isaac: the land whereon thou liest, to thee I will give it, and to thy seed; 14 – And thy seed shall be as the dust of the earth, and thou shall spread abroad to the west, and to the east, and to the north, and to the south: and in thee and in thy seed shall all the families of the earth be blessed. 15 – And, behold, I am with thee, and will keep thee in all places whither thou goest, and will bring thee again into this land; for I will not leave thee, until I have done that which I have spoken to thee of.*

The "he" referred to here is Jacob who was on a journey to find himself a wife, and he dreamed these things as he slept with a stone for a pillow. These memory verses seem to be addressed to the Jewish peoples, since it is directed to the descendants of Isaac and refers to their seed being scattered in all directions, before being reunited in their promised land. The reference to their being a blessing to the earth also fits with the interim history of the Jews. The Arabic peoples have pretty much remained in the deserts of the Mideast and North Africa. The Jewish peoples have traditionally been tradesmen, shopkeepers and entrepreneurs, with notable teachers and scientists including Albert Einstein. The Arabic nations descended from Abraham through Hagar and Ishmael, have fought countless wars among themselves and their neighbors including Israel. In the seven wars conducted by the Arabs against God's chosen people, the scoreboard shows, Jews - 7, Arabs - 0. Reading elsewhere in the Bible, it seems the grand finale war will occur in the Holy Land between the Jews and their foes including the Arabic states, abetted by Russia and China. The Creator of the universe has already announced the winner, and it's the people who were given the land described here in our memory verses.

Exodus 6:4-8 – *And I have also established my covenant with them, to give them the land of Canaan, the land of their pilgrimage, wherein they were strangers. 5 – And I have also heard the groaning of the children of Israel, whom the Egyptians keep in bondage; and I have remembered my covenant. 6 – Wherefore say unto the children of Israel, I am the Lord, and I will bring you out from under the burdens of the Egyptians, and I will rid you out of their bondage, and I will redeem you with a stretched out arm, and with great judgments: 7 – And I will take you to me for a people, and I will be to you a God: and ye shall know that I am the Lord your God, which bringeth you out from under the burdens of the Egyptians. 8 – And I will bring you in unto the land, concerning the which I did swear to give it to Abraham, to Isaac, and to Jacob; and I will give it you for an heritage: I am the Lord.*

These memory verses further identify who God has covenanted with for the land of His promise. It is vastly larger than the thin sliver which encompasses present day Israel. In fact, the Egyptians referred to here are the same country which has figured prominently in collusion with their Arab brothers, in warring against tiny Israel in modern efforts to destroy them.

Exodus 12:13 – *And the blood shall be to you for a token upon the houses where ye are: and when I see the blood, I will pass over you, and the plague shall not be upon you to destroy you, when I smite the land of Egypt.*

In the middle of this memory verse are the two words "pass" and "over" which is where the Jews got the name of their religious holiday, the Passover. This is of course, when they celebrate their release from captivity. The blood of a slain lamb was to be painted on their doorway as a sign to the death angel to pass over the designated houses as he administered death to the firstborn in all of Pharaoh's people. This can be seen as a powerful message showing a parallel with Jesus' shed blood on the cross, and its redemptive action. In neither case it is/was not the action of man that resulted in salvation, but the <u>faith</u> shown in the blood's atonement. It never is any act or work on man's part, but the <u>faith</u> in <u>believing,</u> which brings salvation. This truth is reiterated throughout God's Word, but man is constantly inventing certain ordinances and rituals to allow himself to be empowered in his own redemption. We aren't only powerless to save ourselves, we really can do nothing outside of the power of Christ, just as He told us in John 15:5. We see more references to the atoning power of blood elsewhere as we explore the Scriptures.

Exodus 14:21-23,27,29-31 – *And Moses stretched out his hand over the sea; and the Lord caused the sea to go back by a strong east wind all that night, and made the sea dry land, and the waters were divided. 22 – And the children of Israel went into the midst of the sea upon the dry ground: and the waters were a wall unto them on their right hand, and on their left. 23 – And the Egyptians pursued, and went in after them to the midst of the sea, even all Pharaoh's horses, his chariots, and his horsemen. 27 – And Moses stretched forth his hand over the sea, and the sea returned to his strength when the morning appeared; and the Egyptians fled against it; and the Lord overthrew the Egyptians in the midst of the sea. 29 – But the children of Israel walked upon dry land in the midst of the sea; and the waters were a wall unto them on their right hand, and on their left. 30 – Thus the Lord saved Israel that day out of the hands of the Egyptians; and Israel saw the Egyptians dead upon the sea shore. 31 – And Israel saw that great work which the LORD did upon the Egyptians: and the people feared the LORD, and believed the LORD, and His servant Moses.*

These Scripture segments make a long, rather difficult series for memorization. The omitted verses are somewhat repetitious, while those retained are still much so. We have heard long-winded men's explanations of how God rigged things to make it <u>appear</u> as if the water was parted, etc. Man is forever musing ways to explain biblical events in ways to demote God from His rightful position and elevate man into the resulting vacuum. It is notable that the Israelites didn't stop to ponder the finer points of God's miracle when He provided a safe escape route from the Egyptian army, spearheaded by the elite charioteer troops with blood in their eyes. Those horse-drawn war wagons could move for extended distances at speeds three times faster than a seasoned runner, and about ten times the velocity of women and children with ox-drawn conveyances. It surely took great faith to proceed into the dry pathway with walls of seawater over one hundred feet high on either side. That faith was helped by the hearing of the angry army in hot pursuit. I can accept God's history as He presents it here. We now come to the Decalogue, the Ten Commandments given to Moses by God on Mount Sinai, for the people to observe and live by. This is the basis for our early forefathers' civil and criminal codes. For the readers' convenience, we have placed bold numbers to indicate which Bible verses correspond to each of the Ten Commandments.

1. Exodus 20:3 – *Thou shalt have no other gods before me.* This means Buddha, moon, (either one) sun, stars (either kind), Allah, home, car, money, fame, power, rank, God's Creation including animals, self, family, business, church, sports, recreation, or <u>anything else!</u> In our time, the evil of humanism has morphed into the gods of self and political correctness. **God will not allow His children to do this.**

2. Exodus 20:4 – *Thou shalt not make unto thee any graven image, or any likeness of anything that is in heaven above, or that is in the earth beneath, or that is in the water under the earth:* This is usually interpreted to pertain to pictures and statues which are idols. These things could easily extend to St. Christopher sitting on the dashboard of a car or Buddha there beside him.

Exodus 20:5 – *Thou shalt not bow down thyself to them, nor serve them: for I the Lord thy God am a jealous God, visiting the iniquity of the fathers upon the children unto the third and fourth generation of them that hate me;*

Exodus 20:6 – *And showing mercy unto thousands of them that love me, and keep my commandments.*

These two memory verses serve to establish that this is serious business with our Creator, and that He will punish the miscreants for their sins against Him. His jealousy here refers to His desire for His children to know and obey His rules for them. Also contained in these words from God, is a warning to sinners that He may cause their descendants to suffer for the sins of their forefathers. We may sometimes hear from the pulpit that God doesn't exercise judgment on children for their parents' errors. Those words are just from the pulpit and not from God's Word. The concluding verse assures us that God rewards those who seriously attend to obeying His commandments.

3. Exodus 20:7 – *Thou shalt not take the name of the LORD thy God in vain; for the LORD will not hold him guiltless that taketh His name in vain.*

It is sad to note that this commandment is violated almost universally worldwide, and by all strata of humanity. Belching and picking one's nose are more frowned on in much of modern society than is this ugly, sinful practice. Boys become men and women attain equal status by dragging our God and Savior's name in the mud. Incidentally, did everyone notice that God said He will not hold guiltless those who engage in this vulgar disregard for who He is? The inference seems to be that this infraction of God's law is baggage brought even into Heaven, since He holds His people accountable for it. This admonition is not made concerning the other "thou shalt nots."

4. Exodus 20:8-11 – *Remember the sabbath day, to keep it holy. 9 – Six days shalt thou labour, and do all thy work: 10 – But the seventh day is the sabbath of the Lord thy God: in it thou shalt not do any work, thou, nor thy son, nor thy daughter, thy manservant, nor thy maidservant, nor thy cattle, nor thy stranger that is within thy gates: 11 – For in six days the Lord made heaven and earth, the sea, and all that in them is, and rested the seventh day: wherefore the Lord blessed the sabbath day, and hallowed it.*

Man has more varied opinions regarding this commandment of God than just about anything else contained in Holy Scripture. Modern denominations with the exception of the Seventh Day Adventists have changed the day of rest and worship from what God commanded, to Sunday. They cite a plethora of inane excuses, from Sunday being the day Christ arose, to what the apostle Peter had for breakfast. The real reason is established and recorded in the annals of history. The Roman Catholic church, by decree of the Emperor Constantine, ordered the change in 321 AD to show their power and to differentiate between Christian and Jewish practice. Constantine claimed to be a Christian but he also worshiped the Roman sun god and had a liking for sun day. We will not, I feel, ever change our practice, just please don't call Sunday the sabbath, because it assuredly is not.

5. Exodus 20:12 – *Honour thy father and thy mother: that thy days may be long upon the land which the LORD thy God giveth thee.*

This is the commandment of God with an explicit promise from Him as a reward for our compliance. If we take a little time to study the people we know and have known, we can see the manifestation of this. I grant there are lots of present day parents unworthy of great honor by anyone, including their children, but this commandment of God should encourage us to give honor to them anyway. This situation can be improved if the parents treat the kids with respect too.

6. Exodus 20:13 – *Thou shalt not kill.*

That's short and easy to understand. Of course, this is to be read in the light of the whole counsel of God's Word. We just recently saw where God told the serpent that man would bruise the snake's head. It is normal practice in dealing with rattlesnakes to stand clear of their striking distance and bruise their head with a bullet, rock, or looong handled axe or hoe. It doesn't seem likely that God was including flies, roaches, and bed bugs here. It does on the other hand, seem reasonable He was alluding to other human beings, including babies … especially babies. Our supreme court mocked God in Roe v Wade 35,000,000 babies ago. They are accountable for their mocking God, according to Galatians 6:7. Any applicable exceptions are treated elsewhere in God's Word.

7. Exodus 20:14 – *Thou shalt not commit adultery.*

This is the commandment man has so much humor about. It is popular with too many men around the globe to make a game of seeing how often they can sin in this area and with as many different partners of all sexes without being caught by others, principally their wives. Why this immoral sin is treated so lightly by society is incomprehensible, since it leads directly to so much needless suffering for the practitioners, their families, and society as a whole. This is one practice where mocking God and His law really has a very high price. Among the most unhappy people on this planet, are the ones who thought it was cute of them to run around on their spouse and take another's marriage partner for themselves.

8. Exodus 20:15 – *Thou shalt not steal.*

Our God-given conscience tells us this before we can read the printed word. You could accurately say it is imprinted in our heart before we can read it printed on paper. Stealing from others, anyone, is the antithesis of Christ's Golden Rule, since no one likes to be stolen from. Everyone everywhere shares the desire to not be stolen from. This has been abundantly clear to me personally in my business career, as I have been in the theft control business for over sixty years. Today that small business supports several families, while protecting assets of thousands of burglar alarm customers. Some societies are more tolerant of thieves than others. This is even true among Christian groups. It seems to me that the church of Rome takes a somewhat relaxed view of someone stealing a little for themselves and their family, from an employer or a large company, or just about anyone who has more than you have. That last excuse for stealing intrudes on the tenth commandment which we will examine shortly.

9. Exodus 20:16 – *Thou shalt not bear false witness against thy neighbour.*

Of course, we all know what is meant here. In modern terminology this simply means that we are not to be telling lies to others. Again, this commandment is in direct agreement with Christ's Golden Rule. Do you enjoy having someone tell you a falsehood? Of course not, and neither do I or anyone else. Those who study such things professionally, tell us the average adult in our society tells more than one falsehood every day! That is a shameful statistic and a sad commentary about us.

10. Exodus 20:17 – *Thou shalt not covet thy neighbour's house, thou shalt not covet thy neighbour's wife, nor his manservant, nor his maidservant, nor his ox, nor his ass, nor anything that is thy neighbour's.*

The Reader's Digest Bible (they did print one, I'm told) probably shortened this one to "Don't covet." This sin is universal among human beings, and is a second cousin to that general bane to humanity, <u>pride</u>, and a brother-in-law to selfishness and me-ism. Madison Avenue ad agents make use of our envious nature to sell everything from alarm systems to zoo tickets and everything in between. There is a whole underworld clan of these sinful practices kin to covetousness and they are uniformly ugly. Some of the better known ones are envy, jealousy, selfishness, elitism, greed, stinginess, theft, lying, and cheating. Whenever we covet another's chattel, we open ourselves to a multitude of other devices of the devil. Adam and Eve, in the Garden of Eden coveted the forbidden fruit, and their eldest son Cain coveted the acclaim of God enjoyed by his younger brother Abel. Man's sordid history is strewn with countless other examples from the statehouse to the poorhouse.

Exodus 31:16-17 – *Wherefore the children of Israel shall keep the sabbath, to observe the sabbath throughout their generations, for a perpetual covenant. 17 – It is a sign between me and the children of Israel, for ever: for in six days the Lord made heaven and earth, and on the seventh day he rested, and was refreshed.*

These memory verses somewhat restate the earlier Scripture we recently covered. Just as always though, we see nuggets of truth and wisdom intertwined inside the previously covered matter. For instance, here we see proof in God's own words that He does, indeed, get tired and rests to become refreshed, just as His creatures do.

Leviticus 17:11 – *For the life of the flesh is in the blood: and I have given it to you upon the altar to make an atonement for your souls: for it is the blood that maketh an atonement for the soul.*

This memory verse is just one of the many references throughout the Bible, where we see the connection between blood sacrifice and atonement and redemption. The many such references in the Old

Testament seem to be looking forward to the supreme blood sacrifice of Jesus Christ on Calvary's cross, for the salvation of men's souls. We may not completely understand the thinking of God in such matters, because our thoughts are not His thoughts, as we are told at Isaiah 55:18-19. These things that are not clearly and completely understood now, will be revealed in the light of God's wisdom in eternity, as promised at 1 Corinthians 13:12, where we are promised to have the dark glass removed, that we may see even as He sees.

Leviticus 23:3 – *Six days shall work be done: but the seventh day is a sabbath of rest, an holy convocation; ye shall do no work therein: it is the sabbath of the LORD in all your dwellings.*

When we see these repeated instructions regarding God's sabbath observance, it seems as if the matter was/is important to Him. I recall a men's Sunday School Quarterly of some years ago where it was referred to as "the Jewish sabbath." The Bible refers to it as being God's sabbath for men to observe. We hear many excuses for not obeying God's clear requirement for His sabbath to be observed. "It was just for Israel, it was just part of the ceremonial law, it was done away with, etc." Let's look at the validity of some of these arguments. Weren't the Gentiles grafted in as recorded at Romans 17:11? In the list of over six hundred ceremonial laws there appear only four relating to the sabbath, and they concern how far one could travel etc., not to the general establishment of the day of rest. As far as to the observance being done away with, my question is – by whom? Constantine was emperor of the Roman Empire – not the universe, and Jesus told us at Matthew 5:17, that it wasn't His mission. This fourth commandment seems to be reiterated more than the other nine for some reason.

Numbers 21:8 – *And the Lord said unto Moses, make thee a fiery serpent, and set it upon a pole: and it shall come to pass, that every one that is bitten, when he looketh upon it, shall live.*

The multitude led by Moses in the wilderness for forty years underwent repeated lapses in their faith. They complained a lot, in the King James text, they "murmured" at the slightest provocation. This memory verse refers to a time of troubles where the Israelites had been griping to Moses about the lack of food and water. God sent serpents among the complainers, which had a deadly bite. When those who had been complaining repented of their sins, God gave Moses the dictum we are studying and committing to memory. How often we modern murmurers complain of our lot in life! And how often the Lord sends us a reminder to be thankful for His bounty, and remind us to not murmur. It is usually not as dire as the fiery serpents recounted here, but whenever we are reprimanded we can easily identify it and get with the Lord's program, and enjoy a closer fellowship.

Deuteronomy 6:5-9 – *And thou shalt love the Lord thy God with all thine heart, and with all thy soul, and with all thy might. 6 – And these words, which I command thee this day, shall be in thine heart: 7 – And thou shalt teach them diligently unto thy children, and shalt talk of them when thou sittest in thine house, and when thou walkest by the way, and when thou liest down, and when thou riseth up. 8 – And thou shalt bind them for a sign upon thine hand, and they shall be as frontlets between thine eyes. 9 – And thou shalt write them upon the posts of thy house, and on thy gates.*

This memory Scripture serves to show the minute exactitude with which God issued His instructions for keeping His laws and commandments to His people. And some of us complain when the pastor gently suggests the ladies in the morning services should not expose their belly buttons with their attire! The first memory verse here is a preiteration of Jesus' reply to the lawyer recorded in Matthew 22:37 and Mark 12:30. These verses are mostly addressing walking the walk in everyday living and especially in the sight of our children. God puts a lot of store in how His people comport themselves in conducting their private family lives, and in their public living in the market place, and in commerce. He has always stressed the importance of maintaining a good name ..., for Him and for us.

Joshua 1:8 – *This book of the law shall not depart out of thy mouth; but thou shalt meditate therein day and night, that thou mayest observe to do according to all that is written therein: for then thou shall make thy way prosperous, and then thou shalt have good success.*

Today's mega-church mega-pastors tend to promise their flock and those watching the television broadcast, that they will be blessed abundantly if they will buy the books and dvds, and send a sizable love offering. Sometimes it gets a little blurred as to just exactly who is doing the blessing. I remember hearing Gloria Copeland saying that she and Kenneth were given twin Harley hogs in recognition of something they did or did not do. The promises in the Bible we are considering here place much emphasis on observing and obeying God's laws and precepts.

Joshua 24:15 – *And if it seem evil unto you to serve the Lord, choose you this day whom ye will serve; whether the gods which your fathers served that were on the other side of the flood, or the gods of the Amorites, in whose land ye dwell: but as for me and my house, we will serve the Lord.*

The Amorites don't have much political or commercial heft in our time, but we have plenty of other Baals and Molechs to follow after, which are just as displeasing to the Lord as those were back then. Incidentally, these weird names then and the ones we are about to consider were/are all just masks and aliases for Lucifer-Satan-the devil. The ones we see glorified daily are political correctness-inclusiveness-homosexuals' rights-same sex marriage-a woman's choice, etc. In fact that last one listed here is a sort of extension of ancient Molech. Molech or Moloch was a god with horns like a bull and with his fire-clay hands cupped, to allow a sacrificed baby to be placed in them after they were heated to a molten stage and the baby was burned alive. This is basically what a woman's choice accomplishes today in our society since Roe v Wade. God's Creation still has the choice to serve Him in happiness enroute to heaven, or live in the gutters on our way to hell.

Judges 21:25 – *In those days there was no King in Israel: every man did what was right in his own eyes.*

The political arrangement or condition described here is called anarchy, and it is usually quickly deteriorated into what can be called the law of the jungle. We see flashbacks or short snippets when the authorities sit on their hands and allow the mob to riot in the streets as in the Watts riots of 1965, the Rodney King riots of 1992, and more recent upheavals of public order associated with people or locations and names like Zimmeman, Ferguson and Baltimore. These recent examples of non-action aren't so much that we have no king, as that the king and his head justice have abdicated their responsibilities. The Bible admonishes God's people to obey the laws of the land insomuch as they don't violate God's laws (Acts 5:29). In the Old Testament we see plenty of examples of godless leaders where the repeated phrase is "And King xxxxxx did evil in the sight of the Lord." These periods of no leader or a leader who does the devil's bidding are truly valleys of death to the people. Although God may allow an evil man to become a leader, He is always perfect in His holy leadership Himself. Man is imperfect, but God changes not, and Jesus is the same yesterday, today, and forever (Hebrews 13:8).

Ruth 1:16 – *And Ruth said, entreat me not to leave thee, or to return from following after thee: for whether thou goest, I will go; and where thou lodgest, I will lodge: thy people shall be my people, and thy God my God:*

This beautiful, touching story here pertains to Ruth's loving attachment to her mother-in-law, Naomi, who was preparing to return from Moab to her own country. Naomi was telling Ruth it would be better for Ruth to remain in the country where she was native, the land of her birth. Ruth was adamant that she wanted to stay with her late husband's mother. Read the whole small book of Ruth; it is one of the most pleasant in the entire Bible.

1 Samuel 16:7 – *But the Lord said unto Samuel, look not on his countenance, or on the height of his stature: because I have refused him: for the Lord seeth not as man seeth; for man looketh on the outward appearance, but the Lord looketh on the heart.*

Every personnel director or human resources manager should remember this admonition and refer to Psalm 1 for direction in choosing applicants for jobs. We employ many devices and tests to try to determine the best possible fits to job openings, but it is still pretty hit-or-miss. This passage here is an account of the Lord's selection of David from among the eight brothers, to replace King Saul. David's dad didn't even consider him a candidate, and had not even called him from tending to the sheep to be interviewed! The family head knew them the best of any human, but he still couldn't know even his own sons' hearts like the Lord did.

2 Samuel 22:33 – *God is my strength and power: And He maketh my way perfect.*

This statement by David is still as true and valid for God's people as it was when he said it. This is easy enough to put in the heart so we can have it ready whenever we face obstacles and trials. If a person makes anything or anyone their tower of strength and power, except the One worthy of our trust, they face disappointment and failure.

1 Kings 18:21 – *And Elijah came unto all the people, and said, how long halt ye between two opinions? If the Lord be God, follow Him: but if Baal, then follow him. And the people answered him not a word.*

This memory verse is timed just before God's faithful prophet Elijah, demonstrated the power of God by calling down fire from heaven to consume a burnt offering, after the prophets of Baal had failed to do likewise. Read the whole fascinating account recorded these many centuries ago for us. Then whenever you are reminded of it by facing a problem where diverse courses of action present themselves, you may remember to ask God to reveal His answer to you. I think the reason the people answered Elijah not a word, was because they were undecided, because of the devil's influence in their lives. They were living in a kingdom where the false god Baal (Satan) was worshiped and had 450 false prophets running their religious services. These were abetted by 400 more who "ate at Jezebel's table." This means 400 more false religious leaders who were in the administration of Jezebel and King Ahab. We today in our own country, have our populace divided between two opinions in many different areas. Our present administration has well over 400 false religious leaders inside their tent and the "outside the beltway" false religious leaders surely exceeds 450. Perhaps God will move one or a few true believer leader(s) into prominence and display His awesome power for all to observe. The end of Jezebel recounted here in 1 Kings is descriptive, if you've ever watched a pack of street dogs fighting over fresh, fat road kill.

2 Kings 19:27 – *But I know thy abode, and thy going out, and thy coming in, and thy rage against me.*

These were the words of the Lord delivered by His faithful servant, Isaiah to King Hezekiah. The King was like some of our godless leaders today. He was struttin' his stuff and feeling invincible in his own power. He was thinking of himself, just like we see in the halls of power here today. The message in this memory verse is the equivalent of telling someone who has threatened you and who thinks they are hidden; "I know where you live and where you work." Foolish sinners think they and their evil deeds are hidden and that no one knows where they hide to do their mischief. When I was about three or four years old, my older brother showed me how to climb upon the front of the hood of the family car, a model A Ford. It was pretty lofty to my way of thinking, and well above my reach from the ground. Soon thereafter, our mother had reason to talk to me for something I had done, and when I didn't honor her subpoena she came for me. Remembering just how high that old car hood appeared to me, I made a dash (I <u>could</u> outrun her) and scrambled upon the hood. I then discovered this made my rear end just perfect for mom to administer the switch in her hand vigorously, without having to bend down to do it!

1 Chronicles 29:11 – *Thine, O Lord, is the greatness, and the power, and the glory, and the victory, and the majesty: for all that is in the heaven and in the earth is thine; thine is the kingdom, O Lord, and thou art exalted as head above all.*

This memory verse is recounting King David's prayer following a great outpouring of gifts from the people, as they <u>willingly</u> gave of their bounty to the Lord's service. Everywhere in God's Word, it seems as if the greatest requirements attendant to such giving, are that the act is to always be cheerful and that we not brag about it (2 Corinthians 9:7 & Matthew 6:1-4). There are many more. David was a good king for Israel, even though he was a mediocre husband and a miserable flop as a father to his children. He wrote a large part of the Old Testament, and this Scripture is representative of his best attitude toward his God who called David, "A man after My own heart" (1 Samuel 13:10 & Acts 13:22).

2 Chronicles 7:14 – *If my people, which are called by my name, shall humble themselves, and pray, and seek my face, and turn from their wicked ways; then will I hear from heaven, and will forgive their sin, and will heal their land.*

This is one of my very most favorite memory verses. I have referenced it more in previous books than any other Scripture, I think. It was written in God's Word here as a promise to David and the Israelites, but it stands as a commitment on God's part concerning nations, groups, and individuals, I believe. The very first requirement in obtaining God's favor is that we become **HUMBLE**. Without a show of genuine humility on our part, we can't expect forgiveness from anyone, including the original maker of this statement. After we have humbly presented our petition for forgiveness, we need to come close to the offended party's position and understand their hurt caused by our actions and misdeeds. The whole matter depends on a sincere showing of commitment by our abstaining from repeating our original tort. Someone who repents only to repeat, shows they aren't truthful, but are hypocrites; not worthy of forgiveness. In years past this Scripture has been in my heart and on my lips for our beloved United States of America, and of course all things are possible to God. Now it appears to me that we have probably surpassed the limit of our Maker's patience and have denied Him and His authority beyond any possible redemption. If the Lord should tarry in returning much longer, it seems as if the harvest of those still alive will be small indeed.

Ezra 8:23 – *So we fasted and besought our God for this: and He was entreated of us.*

The king of Babylon had allowed Ezra and his people to return from captivity to Jerusalem. They were transporting much gold and silver and had told the king they had no need for a military escort as they were depending on God for safe passage. At the border River Ahava, they stopped and took the actions indicated here. These events occurred about 450 years before the birth of Jesus. The practice of fasting before and during prayer asking for God's favor, has waned about in the same way buggywhip production has in recent years. It was pleasing to Him back then, and He changes not.

Nehemiah 9:6 – *Thou, even thou, art Lord alone; thou hast made heaven, the heaven of heavens, with all their host, the earth, and all things that are therein, the seas, and all that is therein, and thou preservest them all; and the host of heaven worshippeth thee.*

This is part of a prayer by Ezra over fifty years after the preceding memory verse. He is still toiling in Jerusalem putting things back in order for the return of the last exiles. He is acknowledging God as all-powerful and the Creator of the universe and everything it contains. This great man of God had witnessed innumerable miracles during his long lifetime and was giving his witness to them here. As we see God do great things in our lives, it would be good to take time (which time comes from Him) to thank Him for every blessing we receive from His outstretched arm.

Esther 4:14 – For *if thou altogether holdest thy peace at this time, then shall there enlargement and deliverance arise to the Jews from another place; but thou and thy father's house shall be destroyed: and who knoweth whether thou art come to the kingdom for such a time as this?*

This is the Scripture I referred to earlier which was the memory verse assigned to the old men's class in that Fort Worth church years ago. The person speaking here is Queen Esther's cousin, Mordecai, who raised her as a daughter. The king had been duped into decreeing death to all Jews living in Persia, and it befell Esther to petition the king to spare her and her people. This is one of the most intriguing stories in the Bible. It has all the trappings of a well-written mystery novel. It is even sited in modern day Iran, where the people still live by mistreating each other and are still killing Jews, and now Christians as well, as they prepare, with our administration's help, to develop atomic warhead armed ICBMs targeting Tel Aviv and Washington, DC.

Job 5:7 – *Yet man is born unto trouble, as the sparks fly upward.*

Do you ever ask yourself why you tend to have so many problems as you try to make it through the day? I guess we all do that, and here's the answer from a man who had more troubles before breakfast than most of us experience in our entire lifetime. Several years, ago my wife Shirley and I were at our place near El Remolino, Mexico, and were watching as some mesquite logs were staging a fireworks display in the large fireplace in the casita. We were familiar with this memory verse passage here, but at that time, weren't able to find it in our Bible. We called our good friend, Gene Petitt in Del Rio on the radiophone and, Gene quickly told us where it is in the Bible. In later years, when we were able to relax in front of that big fireplace and the sparks began to fly up the chimney, we were reminded of that happy occasion. It is brought back to us now when we are reciting memory verses, and we come to Job 5:7. The story of Job in the Bible is one of the most unusual stories of "bad luck" ever recorded. Read it and see luck had nothing to do with it.

Job 14:14 – *If a man die, shall he live again? All the days of my appointed time will I wait, till my change come.*

Job was posing a question here that he surely had good insight as to the answer. He was/had been a wealthy man and one the Lord counted as being perfect as recorded in the book's opening passage. Satan was allowed by God to torment Job mercilessly and take his family and his wealth. To me, this is one of the Bible's most depressing and most encouraging stories. Read it, and the next time you rush out of the house to attend to some important duty before it's too late and find your car with a flat tire and a dead battery, you can just smile and say, "Well, at least this isn't too bad when compared with the tribulations of God's servant Job!"

Job 14:15 – *Thou shalt call. And I will answer thee: thou wilt have a desire to the work of thine hands.*

This is a showing of Job's understanding of God's interest in what Job is doing ..., both good and bad. Job is saying he knows God sees all, and Job wants a close walk with Him.

Job 19:23-27 – *Oh that my words were now written! oh that they were printed in a book! 24 – That they were graven with an iron pen and lead in the rock forever! 25 – For I know that my redeemer liveth, and that he shall stand at the latter day upon the earth: 26 – And though after my skin worms destroy this body, yet in my flesh shall I see God: 27 – Whom*

I shall see for myself, and mine eyes shall behold, and not another; though my reins be consumed within me.

This Scripture – these memory verses display a very deep understanding of the processes undergone by our physical bodies after we pass from this vale of tears, to be redeemed in bodies of perfection with our Creator in Heaven. Job was not only blameless in God's eyes …, he had great wisdom instilled by God also.

Job 23:10 – But He *knoweth the way that I take: when He hath tried me, I shall come forth as gold.*

Job is repeating the words of assurance given to him earlier by God. He was doing so at a time of great testing, as he was passing through a deeper valley than most of us will ever be asked to endure.

Job 26:7 – *He stretcheth out the north over the empty place, and hangeth the earth upon nothing.*

God's perfect servant Job, had a great understanding, even extending into astronomy. The later men of that science – Ptlomey – Copernicus – Galileo, could have used Job's observations to start them in the right direction. This reminds us that all knowledge and wisdom worth our while comes from the One who created us and everything else.

Psalm 1 – *Blessed is the man that walketh not in the counsel of the ungodly, nor standeth in the way of sinners, nor sitteth in the seat of the scornful. 2 – But his delight is in the law of the Lord; and in His law doth he meditate day and night. 3 – And he shall be like a tree planted by the rivers of water, that bringeth forth his fruit in his season; his leaf also shall not wither; and whatsoever he doeth shall prosper. 4 – The ungodly are not so: but are like the chaff which the wind driveth away. 5 – Therefore the ungodly shall not stand in the judgement, nor sinners in the congregation of the righteous. 6 – For the Lord knoweth the way of the righteous: but the way of the ungodly shall perish.*

This is the memory Scripture I referred to earlier, as that which the gentleman at the Canton Trade Days was exhibiting. He was correct in saying the first half was/is the "good" part. I never gave much notice to the character clues given by those I was involving myself and my family with, when choosing partners in business arrangements. We all paid a price a few times because of my errors. The people to avoid listed in verse one can cause more trouble than they are worth sometimes. A good rule is to avoid entanglements with people who brag and boast about themselves and their accomplishments. That seems to be the people who win political office in too many races. The verse relating the observance of God's law is instructional. We can all benefit from remembering and emulating that. This memory Scripture is my personal "factory default setting," when I encounter a forced waiting period that looks as if it will be extended; this passage comes to my mind first. It appeases our sense of justice when we see ungodly, sinful people running roughshod over weaker ones, to recall the closing sentence, knowing they have a day of reckoning coming at the hand of the God who will not be mocked.

Psalm 8:3-9 – *When I consider thy heavens, the work of thy fingers, the moon and the stars, which thou hast ordained; 4 – What is man, that thou art mindful of him? And the son of man, that thou visiteth him? 5 – For thou hath made him a little lower than the angels, and hast crowned him with glory and honor. 6 – Thou madest him have dominion over the works of thine hands: thou hast put all things under his feet: 7 – All sheep and oxen, yea, and the beast of the field; 8 – The fowl of the air, and the fish of the sea, and whatsoever passeth through the paths of the seas. 9 – O Lord our Lord, how excellent is thy name in all the earth!*

The Psalmist had a good understanding of the universe, as we discussed earlier of Job. Here he starts his adoring poetry by saying how we should feel when observing and admiring God's mighty work which surrounds our earth on all sides. He then asks (in comparison to the universe) "What is man?" In other words, what is the value or significance of puny humanity compared to the cosmos. He then establishes that man is positioned in God's inventory just under the angels of Heaven and above and in charge of all other animal life. That position given to us by the Creator of all things, is the reason we eat hamburgers, while the Hindus of India have cows impeding traffic, while some of their people are starving. The misguided members of PETA and others who eschew meat, don't believe the message from God through David, given to us here for our guidance.

Psalm 12:8 – *The wicked walk on every side, when the vilest men are exalted.*

Every time we hear someone questioning the sanity of our godless political leaders, we could easily and accurately quote this short, simple, and effective memory verse. The empowering of a vile regime historically brings the most wicked people into all areas of government. They seem to inundate us, to "walk on every side," as they drown the people in wicked programs, to subjugate the citizens and keep the evil ones in power. We have a secular saying, "Birds of a feather flock together." Well, looking at our politicians of today, the same can be said of cockroaches and rattlesnakes. Even the low level job of tax administrator can be ill-affected by evil leadership, into treating the taxpayers who pay his wages like they were dirt. It's not one of our memory verses, but perhaps it should be as it echoes this one, Proverbs 28:19 says, *Where there is no vision, the people perish; but he that keepeth the law, happy is he.* We should not depend on flesh and blood (mankind), but on the strong arm of God.

Psalm 19:14 – *Let the words of my mouth, and the meditation of my heart, be acceptable in thy sight, O Lord, my strength, and my redeemer.*

This is a request to God for His help in our guardianship of what we say and think about. Most of us were reared to not be using dirty language in front of our parents, and that is good … as far as it goes. More importantly, we should be even more circumspect in what God hears from us. He not only hears our words, He knows the thoughts of our hearts and minds. They are/were our parents – He is our everlasting strength and Redeemer. This short memory verse would be an excellent prayer each morning as we arise to greet the day He has provided for us.

Psalm 20:7 – *Some trust in chariots, and some in horses: but we will remember the name of the Lord our God.*

In the days of David, the military field commanders rode war chariots pulled by the best horses. These commanders were surrounded by horse mounted spearmen and bowmen. Here in this poetic memory verse, David is reminding us that men, chariots, and horses have their natural limits, while the strong arm of God never fails. He had ample battlefield experience to make this Word of God to also have validity as a human observation. When we enter into earthly battles, it is assuring to have well-trained, seasoned troops with the best arms and armor. It is vastly more important to have the blessings of God in your favor.

Psalm 22:14-18 – *I am poured out like water, and all my bones are out of joint: my heart is like wax; it is melted in the midsts of my bowels. 15 – My strength is dried up like a potsherd; and my tongue cleaveth to my jaws; and thou hast brought me into the dust of death. 16 – For dogs have compassed me: the assembly of the wicked have enclosed me: they pierced my hands and my feet. 17 – I may tell all my bones: they look and stare upon me. 18 – They part my garments among them, and cast lots upon my vesture.*

This prophesy of David here, is a perfect preview of the crucifixion of Jesus Christ made centuries before the establishment of the Roman Empire and their invention of this most painful and barbaric form of killing human beings. Notice the poetic reference to the pain and shame of the occasion. One would think only the person undergoing the degradation and discomfort could so well describe the human feelings of this horrible experience. Jesus died on that cross for our salvation as, a man Himself. His Deity never lapsed; He died as a man – then he arose as man and God. The psalmist had the minute details revealed to him by God, even down to the Roman soldiers casting lots, (throwing dice) for Jesus' seamless robe!

Psalm 23 – *The Lord is my shepherd; I shall not want. 2 – He maketh me to lie down in green pastures: He leadeth me beside the still waters. 3 – He restoreth my soul: He leadeth me in the paths of righteousness for His name's sake. 4 – Yea, though I walk through the valley of the shadow of death, I will fear no evil: for thou art with me; thy rod and thy staff they comfort me. 5 – Thou preparest a table before me in the presence of mine enemies: Thou annointest my head with oil; my cup runneth over. 6 – Surely goodness and mercy shall follow me all the days of my life: and I will dwell in the house of the Lord for ever.*

This most beautiful, soothing and reassuring poem of our Lord, is heard at most Christian funerals; it deserves much wider acclaim and recitation. The efforts of our modern Bible re-translators to improve the message and meter of this beloved poem of hope dismay me. Their end product is about what you would get, if you gave a Ferrari sports car to some neighborhood kids with a metal saw and welder and expected them to enhance the vehicle's styling and performance. To spend a million dollars changing the words in the Bible, identifies people with nothing worthwhile to do. To have them alter the closing words from, *and I will dwell in the house of the Lord forever,* to say, "I will dwell in the house of the Lord as long as I live," is sadly ignorant of the concept of God's promises of eternity.

Psalm 27:1 – *The Lord is my light and my salvation; whom shall I fear? the Lord is the strength of my life; of whom shall I be afraid?*

The questions posed here in this memory verse are already answered in reams of Scripture, and the reply, of course is NO ONE. There is a unique strength and sense of assurance in knowing one is engaged in an effort where one is protected by the shield of God's righteous approval. These words will become more reassuring and supportive to Christians as we see the evil head of Islam enslaving and murdering our people in the years to come. That evil head is the same one identified in the memory verse at Genesis 3:15, where I understand that Jesus will crush it. May God's elect go forth into battle with Psalm 27:1 as their battle cry.

Psalm 32:8 – *I will instruct thee and teach thee in the way which thou shalt go: I will guide thee with mine eye.*

This short, easily understood and supportive memory verse of Scripture is a solemn promise from our Creator and Savior to impart His wisdom and knowledge to us for our benefit under His ever watchful supervision. Proverbs 2:6-7, somewhat echoes and buttresses this Scripture, and James 1:5 tells us this is a gift from the Lord that we should specifically request in order to obtain it.

Psalm 37:4-5 – *Delight thyself also in the Lord; and He shall give thee the desires of thine heart. 5 – Commit thy way unto the Lord; trust also in Him; and He shall bring it to pass.*

This memory Scripture is an early stating of truth which is reiterated somewhat in other passages, notably in Matthew, chapters 6 and 7. The passage at Matthew 7:7; is especially poignant here, and we plan to study it in more depth when we get there later. Verse 5 here gives us His assurance that if we tell Him of our plans in prayer, He will see the project through to completion.

Psalm 42:11 – *Why art thou cast down, O my soul? and why art thou disquieted within me? hope thou in God: for I shall yet praise Him, who is the health of my countenance, and my God.*

Here the psalmist questions his innermost being as to why he is feeling low and morose, even though he has the hope (assurance) of God. He then reminds himself that God is all …,all he needs. We tend to think that since God knows our heart, we needn't vocalize the fact. It is for <u>our</u> benefit that we need to reiterate our dependence on Him for our very existence.

Psalm 46:10 – *Be still, and know that I am God: I will be exalted among the heathen, I will be exalted in the earth.*

We don't have to be well-studied Bible scholars to know this truth. If we will just shut our mouths and think of the many, many ways we have of knowing of His existence, we all have an innate sense of His presence. Even the uneducated, ignorant, indigenous people in the deepest wilderness can know of His presence in the earth. This verse of Scripture is a favorite of poets and songwriters. One beautiful such song has the first eight words as its title. It was written by a man named Stephen Curtis Chapman.

Psalm *51:10 – Create in me a clean heart, O God; and renew a right spirit within me.*

The clean heart spoken of here is the heart of flesh God gives us to replace the hard heart we have when we come to Him for salvation. We see this theme elsewhere in the Bible; two such places are in the book of Ezekiel, at 11:19 and 36:26. The way the closing sentence asks God to renew a right spirit, seems to suggest a previous condition of having had a right spirit. Could we understand David was speaking of his/our spirit as babes, before the years of accountability?

Psalm 103:12 – *As far as the east is from the west, so far hath He removed our transgressions from us.*

This truth of God is sprinkled throughout His Word. Here it is displayed in geographic terms that are impressive to us. Consider it; if one goes north far enough, at the North Pole the continued course becomes south until the South Pole is attained. On the contrary, when you start going either east or west, if you continue, it is never changing. The meaning of our memory verse is <u>total separation</u>. God can do this because He can do anything He desires. Human beings, on the other hand, aren't able to easily, completely forget anything. When we forgive another for wrongs done, we don't usually forget entirely. When God forgives, it is completely forgotten, never to be dragged up for further consideration. Isn't this promise a comfort, coming from our Judge?

Psalm 113:3 – *From the rising of the sun unto the going down of the same the Lord's name is to be praised.*

This short memory verse is a reminder of who the Lord is, and how we should ever be in praise of His name; the name that is above every name! It is also an invitation to revere His name, to not be taking it in vain, and to *pray without ceasing.* Typing this Scripture into the word processor, I noticed it is one of the longest sentences in the KJV, with no punctuation marks save the closing period and apostrophe in Lord's.

Psalm 116:12-17 – *What shall I render unto the Lord for all His benefits toward me?*

This question is still very prevalent among religious people. We humans don't want to be beholden to anyone for anything. This human characteristic is simple, selfish pride. We all want to "pay my own way." Although it is made abundantly clear throughout Scripture, that our salvation is a free gift from God, we tend to want to "do something" - something like be baptized, perform some rite, or undergo some training …, or something. 13 – *I will take the cup of salvation, and call upon the name of the Lord.* We <u>can</u> receive the cup of salvation – the free offering from Him. When we "call upon the name of the Lord" we are thanking Him for His sacrifice on the cross for our redemption. There are no works indicated here – only thankful acceptance. 14 – *I will pay my vows to the Lord now in the presence of all His people.* The use of the word "pay" here doesn't imply payment of an obligation, but as in paying respects or paying a compliment etc. We should all pay our vows to Him forever, for His blood gift from the cross. 15 – *Precious in the sight of the Lord is the death of His saints.* When we die to our lives here on earth, we are present in Heaven with the Lord and His angels. This is of course, a joyous occasion for everyone there. 16 – *O Lord, truly I am thy servant; I am thy servant, and the son of thy handmaid: Thou hast loosed my bonds.* In our service to Him we are freed of all other encumbrances. 17 – *I will offer to Thee the sacrifice of thanksgiving, and will call upon the name of the Lord.* Here is the proper return gift. Not "Look what I did," but "Look what Jesus Christ did for me!" And He stands ready to do the same for everyone who believes on Him.

Psalm 118:24 – *This is the day which the Lord hath made; we will rejoice and be glad in it.*

One morning a few years ago, I walked into the office and noticed everyone I greeted was somewhat subdued and reticent in their greetings. Standing in the hallway near three occupied offices, with open doors, I loudly proclaimed this memory verse …; it was September 11, 2001. Those present were all good friends, as well as company employees. They quietly announced the news to me, as I had not heard of the evil attack on our country by the forces of Islam. Perhaps my announcement of the Scripture was inappropriate, or ill-timed. It was, however in my estimation, an accurate depiction of how we are to evaluate every new day. That was/is a day of infamy, much like December 7, 1941 both dates were the day our country was forced to recognize our deadly enemy. This enemy is Satan, operating through the Nazis and Islam. The truth is, many times the day of bad news may also be a day God made for an eventual blessing.

Psalm 119:11 – *Thy word have I hid in mine heart, that I might not sin against Thee.*

This is the title Scripture, the title memory verse, which announces the core message for this book. It designates where we are to keep (hide) God's Word, not just in our memory cells in our brain, but first in our hearts. Head knowledge of God's instructions cannot have everlasting effect, but His Word held as a key conviction leads to repentance and salvation. His Word is pure truth – the truth that sets us free! Put a few of God's words in memory and in your heart. I promise you, you will benefit from it.

Psalm 119:105 - *Thy word is a lamp unto my feet, and a light unto my path.*

This is a very short verse, and with short words. The word "light" being the only one with more than four letters. They are all only one syllable, except "unto," and easy to pronounce. In spite of all this, I continued to get the words "lamp" and "light" confused for some reason. The thing that helped me get over that was Shirley's pointing out that a lamp is short-range, just as a step by one's foot is, while a light suggests a beam projected forward to light a pathway. We all need both kinds of illumination in making life's selections. We need to know where the next step is to be, and the long range path to our ultimate goal. We need to please the Lord in each step we take, in order to reach our heavenly home.

Psalm 139:23-24 – *Search me, O God, and know my heart: try me, and know my thoughts: 24 – And see if there be any wicked way in me, and lead me in the way everlasting.*

Here the psalmist invites the Holy Creator to give him a spiritual safety check, and a road map for trip planning. We should strive to live our lives close to God, knowing we cannot hide our thoughts or actions from Him. The closing words are asking Him to show by His leadership, the strait gate – the way we should go. Go to reach our heavenly rewards.

Psalm 145:8-9 – *The Lord is gracious, and full of compassion; slow to anger, and of great mercy. 9 – The Lord is good to all: and His tender mercies are over all His works.*

We are told elsewhere in the Bible that God is love. Here we see the excellent word-smithing of His Holy Spirit through the words of the psalmist telling the same message without even using the word, love. What beautiful poetry – what a beautiful message.

Proverbs 3:5-6 – *Trust in the Lord with all thine heart; and lean not unto thine own understanding. 6 – In all thy ways acknowledge Him, and He shall direct thy paths.*

Careful attention to this Scripture would save God's people from a multitude of errors every day. We make great plans, get everything together to do things our way …,then have a last-minute, short prayer asking His blessings on our plans. How dismissive we tend to be of our strongest asset to good management and order! We tear off on a wild tangent, then when the funds aren't covering costs, or time starts to run out, we remember to ask Him to bail us out. How juvenile, how simple minded of us. The closing thought tells us we should acknowledge His place in our lives in order to receive His recommended routing through the strait gate to life eternal.

Proverbs 9:10 – *The fear of the Lord is the beginning of wisdom: and the knowledge of the holy is understanding.*

The fear cited here is not dread nor terror, but awe and worship. This exact thought is expressed at other locations in the Bible. Google the words and see what I mean. If we are in awe of God and His precepts we will naturally desire to share in His wisdom. All we need do, as His children, is make a humble request and He, as a good Father delights in giving good gifts unto His children.

Proverbs 13:1 – *A wise son heareth his father's instruction: but a scorner heareth not rebuke.*

The message here for us is that smart people listen to their elders, even when the message to them isn't all compliments and praise. We all accept praise, even if it's not earned, but few can bide a little criticism, even well-meant and coming from friends or family. Kids should listen to the old folks. Grown kids really should listen to them.

Proverbs 13:18 – *Poverty and shame shall be to him that refuseth instruction: but he that regardeth reproof shall be honoured.*

This passage is rather a restatement of the foregoing memory verse. It reveals the same basic truths rendered in different wording. This verse mentions the shame associated with the induced poverty and makes it a general declaration, not connected with family relations.

Proverbs 14:12 – *There is a way which seemeth right unto a man, but the ends thereof are the ways of death.*

This little memory verse has a big message. It cautions us that the course we take can be perilous when we just rely on our human judgment without consulting God's recommendations. Just because it <u>seems</u> right doesn't always prove out to <u>be</u> right.

Proverbs 22:1 – *A good name is rather to be chosen than great riches, and loving favour rather than silver and gold.*

This memory verse is dear to my heart. It has been displayed at the business offices for over a quarter of a century. That business has progressed well and grown for over sixty years, by God's grace. It enjoys a sterling reputation in the community and the areas where we operate. People and businesses trust our company and the individuals who make it run smoothly and effectively. We realize this can all be taken from us by a single bad choice. Incidentally, it appears silver and gold were standards of value a long while ago.

Proverbs 22:6 – *Train up a child in the way he should go: and when he is old, he will not depart from it.*

This observation is to encourage parents and teachers to train children as they are growing up into adulthood. I recall an older aunt, who was experiencing some difficulties with a young, grown son saying: "well that isn't much help before he gets old." I must add, "he" didn't improve with more aging, so maybe the early training (during a divorce of his parents) was somewhat lacking.

Proverbs 28:1 – *The wicked flee when no man pursueth: but the righteous are bold as a lion.*

People who are engaged in evil deeds tend to be paranoid, caused by their God-given conscience. Conversely, someone who has a genuinely clear conscience is not intimidated by legal inquiry. Sometimes guilty persons affect a bravado act when confronted regarding something shady in their operations. The well trained, intuitive investigator is seldom fooled by such ..., and God never is.

Proverbs 29:1 – *He, that being often reproved hardeneth his neck, shall suddenly be destroyed, and that without remedy.*

This speaks of the hard-headed individual who just gets more stiff-necked when corrected about some error he has committed. These dense persons are destroyed by losing one good position after another. Pity the wife and children of these people who have too high opinions of themselves. The closing comment, *and that without remedy,* speaks to the fact that these afflicted individuals often go to their graves, still stiff-necked and unlearning.

Ecclesiastes 3:1 – *To everything there is a season, and a time to every purpose under the heaven:*

This memory verse has been in my ears longer than any other, because it was repeated many times by my own mother talking to her children. The popular rendition, likely by people who aren't familiar with its roots is; "There's a time and a place for everything." This is often followed by; "And this ain't the time or place for that." Read the rest of the chapter. The next eight verses list a lot of different times to do alternating, opposing things.

Song of Solomon 8:7 – *Many waters cannot quench love, neither can the floods drown it: if a man would give all the substance of his house for love, it would utterly be contemned.*

That last word there, contemned, isn't one we see every day; it means disliked, hated, scorned. This is only one of scores of places where the unique value of love is championed.

Isaiah 1:18 – *Come now, and let us reason together, sayeth the Lord: though your sins be as scarlet, they shall be as white as snow; though they be red like crimson, they shall be as wool.*

For some reason beyond my understanding, this favorite verse of many preachers is also often misquoted by transposing the red – crimson and snow – wool words. I heard one pastor refer to it several times over years of preaching, and he got it wrong every time. In one of his published sermons, the "prince of preachers" Charles Spurgeon got it wrong. That was some 150 years ago and a recent printing by Baker still has it wrong. The message, even if it is mixed up, is a great truth for us today.

Isaiah 7:14 – *Therefore the Lord himself shall give you a sign; behold, a virgin shall conceive, and bear a son, and shall call His name Immanuel.*

This prophesy by Isaiah was made some 700 years before the birth of Jesus foretold here. People scratched their heads for all those years. Not only that, the Jewish religious leaders of the time of the Savior's birth were still scratching their heads, just as they do even today! Jesus' mother, Mary understood; she obeyed the angel of the Lord's instructions and called the infant Immanuel – which means, "God with us."

Isaiah 29:13 – Wherefore *the Lord said, forasmuch as this people draw near me with their mouth, and with their lips do honour me, but have removed their heart far from me, and their fear toward me is taught by the precept of men:*

These are the pious acting people, who "talk the talk" but don't "walk the walk." They join a church with the same motivation that they join the country club or the rod and reel group – to be included with their friends whom they admire. These poor things can easily fool most of us, but God knows their hearts. Their souls are precious to the Lord, and He wants them to stop playing head games before their demise here and their arrival in eternity. We can discuss these serious issues without accusing them of being wolves-in-sheep skins.

Isaiah 40:8 – *The grass withereth, the flower fadeth: but the word of our God shall stand forever.*

Thank God for His promise here. This means the Bible burners can never prevail, and that the authority of it will never fade! This is just one such assurance in His Word, it is reiterated elsewhere.

Isaiah 40:31 – *But they that wait upon the Lord shall renew their strength; they shall mount up with wings as eagles; they shall run, and not be weary; and they shall walk, and not faint.*

This is a strong case for the practice of reasonable rest in times of labor. I was raised on a West Texas cotton farm. My dad must have skipped this memory verse. I know why, and understood it back then, but it seemed as if quitting time would never come on some of those long, hot, summer days, hoeing half-mile cotton rows. Realistically, sometimes we just need to take a break and consider what needs our attention most.

Isaiah 53:3-12 – *He is despised and rejected of men; a man of sorrows, and acquainted with grief: and we hid as it were our faces from Him; He was despised, and we esteemed Him not. 4- Surely He hath borne our griefs, and carried our sorrows: yet we did esteem Him stricken, smitten of God, and afflicted. 5 – But He was wounded for our transgressions, He was bruised for our iniquities: the chastisement of our peace was upon Him; and with His stripes we are healed. 6 – All we like sheep have gone astray; we have turned every one to his own way; and the Lord hath laid on Him the inequity of us all. 7 – He was oppressed, and He was afflicted, yet He opened not His mouth: he was brought as a lamb to the slaughter, and as a sheep before her shearers is dumb, so He openeth not His mouth. 8 – He was taken from prison and from judgment: and who shall declare His generation? for He was cut off out of the land of the living: for the transgressions of my people was he stricken. 9 – And He made His grave with the wicked, and with the rich in His death; because He had done no violence, neither was any deceit in His mouth. 10 – Yet it pleased the Lord to bruise Him; He hath put Him to grief: when thou shalt make His soul an offering for sin, He shall see His seed, He shall prolong His days, and the pleasure of the Lord shall prosper in His hand. 11 – He shall see of the travail of His soul, and shall be satisfied: by His knowledge shall my righteous servant justify many; for He shall bear their iniquities. 12 – Therefore will I divide Him a portion with the great, and He shall divide the spoil with the strong; because He hath poured out*

His soul unto death: and He was numbered with the transgressors; and He bare the sins of many, and made intercession for the transgressors.

This Scripture is one of the longer passage we memorized and one of the most difficult because the similar verses lend themselves to being hard to not get off on the wrong line. The messages contained in this exceptional narrative are many, and continue to make themselves manifest with each re-reading. This is another very accurate description of the trials and pains Jesus underwent in the Roman kangaroo court seven centuries after Isaiah wrote this prophesy. It is hard to understand how His own people could deny Him when His coming had been foretold by the different men of God over and over. Read this again tomorrow and in days to come. The different truths that present themselves as you commit it to memory is amazing.

Isaiah 55:8-11 – *For my thoughts are not your thoughts, neither are your ways my ways, saith the Lord. 9 – For as the heavens are higher than the earth, so are my ways higher than your ways, and my thoughts than your thoughts. 10 – For as the rain cometh down, and the snow from heaven, and returneth not thither, but watereth the earth, and maketh it bring forth and bud, that it may give seed to the sower, and bread to the eater: 11 – So shall my word be that goeth forth out of my mouth: it shall not return unto me void, but it shall accomplish that which I please, and it shall prosper in the thing whereto I sent it.*

Here is yet another Scripture telling us that God preserves His Word. It also impresses us with the truth that God doesn't think nor act like we do. What a great blessing that is! The marvelous mechanics established by God, the so called rain cycle is hinted at as well.

Jeremiah 17:7-8 – *Blessed is the man that trusteth in the Lord, and whose hope the Lord is. 8 -for he shall be as a tree planted by the waters, and that spreadeth out her roots by the river, and shall not see when heat cometh, but her leaf shall be green; and shall not be careful in the year of drought, neither shall cease from yielding fruit.*

This Scripture reminds us of the wording and thought seen in Psalm 1:3. Both picture a person who trusts in the Lord and compares them to a tree planted by water where there is plenty of nutrients to sustain the tree which produces abundant amounts of fruit and seeds for propagation. Men and trees are compared elsewhere in the Bible. Both stand upright if healthy, and both require God's provision in order to produce their expected fruit.

Jeremiah 33:3 – *Call unto me, and I will answer thee, and shew thee great and mighty things, which thou knowest not.*

We have seen trucks on the highway with the numbers identifying this memory verse with the notation: "God's telephone number." This Scripture is a promise that God will reveal great truths and impart His wisdom to those who prayerfully call to Him to fill their needs.

Lamentations 3:22 – *It is of the Lord's mercies that we are not consumed, because His compassions fail not.*

This short memory verse is a reminder that without Him we are powerless. This truth is reiterated at John 15:3b. Except for His mercy we would all be done away with – consumed in the fires of hell. As we see in Matthew 7:19 and John 15:6 unworthy men and tree branches are cast into the fire where they burn up – are consumed.

Ezekiel 12:2 – *Son of man, thou dwellest in the midst of a rebellious house, which have eyes to see, and see not; they have ears to hear, and hear not: for they are a rebellious house.*

Here is the account of what the Lord told the prophet Ezekiel he should do when the good prophet was living among people who had an opportunity to know God's desires for them. These people had access to God's instructions for them, but they chose to ignore His rules for them and their innate consciences and go their own way serving themselves, their lusts, and evil pleasures. These instructions are operable to God's people today when they find themselves in a church that eschews the blood-earned redemption of Jesus, and turn to <u>any other</u> watered down substitute, progressive "gospel."

Daniel 3:24-25 – *Then Nebuchadnezzar the king was astonied, and rose up in haste, and spake, and said unto his counselors, Did not we cast three men bound into the midst of the fire? They answered and said unto the king, True, O king. 25 – He answered and said, Lo, I see four men loose, walking in the midst of the fire, and they have no hurt; and the form of the fourth is like the Son of God.*

Isn't this an astounding account of a supernatural occurrence here? They had the fire so hot in there that the soldiers who threw the three friends of Daniel into the fire were themselves killed by the extreme heat. I have sometimes complained about new-age Bibles that change words to fit the writer's agenda. To see a good example of this sinful practice check out this account in one of those books. One large denomination spent one million dollars of the faithful's money to produce their new age edition. Here's how those people re-arranged the closing words here. "… and the fourth looks like a son of the gods." Some others say "a son of a god." Those tempted to add to or take away words of the Bible should read the penalties proscribed for such sinful acts as recorded in the closing verses of the Bible.

Hosea 14:9 – *Who is wise, and he shall understand these things? Prudent, and he shall know them? For the ways of the Lord are right, and the just shall walk in them: but the transgressors shall fall therein.*

Another Scripture avowing protection the Lord provides for His elect, and the fact that sinners shall be denied. The Bible is replete with such promises and warnings. The wise referred to here are those with wisdom, and all true wisdom comes from God.

Joel 2:28 – *And it shall come to pass afterward, that I will pour out my spirit upon all flesh; and your sons and your daughters shall prophesy, your old men shall dream dreams, your young men shall see visions:*

Are there really women prophets? Apparently so, according to this Scripture. I used to wonder what the difference between dreams and visions were. Now, having experienced the visions of mountains climbed and rivers crossed, of having a family and running a business etc., and now, looking back at all that and remembering – dreaming of it, I understand. Thank the Lord for those future visions of youth and the remembering dreams of old age.

Amos 8:11 – *Behold, the days come, sayeth the Lord God, that I will send a famine in the land, not a famine of bread, nor a thirst for water, but of hearing the words of the Lord.*

When I first remember reading this little verse years ago, I wondered when and how such a thing could ever come to pass in our great nation. Now we need wonder no more. The day is at hand, we are seeing it every day. The "words of the Lord" His Bible is now banned from our halls of education, military chaplain's desks, government offices, and many public forums. Where allowed, the versions used in many modern churches deny the Deity of Jesus Christ, don't mention the blood of His cross, and call Father God something reminiscent of mother goose. In many progressive churches one can sit through sermons that contain physcobabble, social programs, feel good, warm fuzzy, self-image junk, without the Bible even being referred to. The great old church structures of England and Europe are being vacated, and turned into museums, bars or Islamic mosques. The days prophesied in Amos 8:11 are no longer future – we are living in those times <u>NOW</u>!

Obadiah 1:4 – *Though thou exalt thyself as the eagle, and though thy set thy nest among the stars, thence will I bring thee down, saith the Lord.*

This reminds me of the story recounted earlier of my safe aerie on the old car's hood. Although man brags (exalts himself) and fancies himself as something marvelous, God sees directly through all this subterfuge and posturing. Except through loving God with our all, and loving our neighbor, man is really just a couple of dollars' worth of greasy minerals – lower than a snake's belly really.

Jonah 2:1-2 – *Then Jonah prayed unto the Lord his God out of the fish's belly. And said, I cried by reason of mine affliction unto the Lord, and He heard me; out of the belly of hell cried I, and thou heardest my voice.*

We may have times and areas where our cell phone doesn't work very well, but thank the Lord He is available from anywhere – even inside a big fish down in the depths of the sea. When Jonah repented for his sin of disobedience God graciously forgave him, had him deposited ashore and then gave him a glorious victory with the souls of Nineveh. God will never leave us nor forsake us. We can distance ourselves from Him – but He always knows where we are!

Micah 5:2 – *But thou, Bethlehem Ephratah, though thou be little among the thousands of Judah, yet out of thee shall He come forth unto me that is to be ruler in Israel; whose goings forth have been from of old, from everlasting.*

The location for Jesus' birth was established centuries prior to its happening. Humans would naturally have chosen some high dollar location in an important major city, perhaps the capitol or main center or commerce. At least a newer four or five star hotel, in the presidential suite, of course. God doesn't operate like men do. Here the prophet Micah is pinpointing the location over 700 years before it occurred.

Micah 6:8 – *He hath showed thee, O man, what is good; and what doth the Lord require of thee, but to do justly, and to love mercy, and to walk humbly with thy god?*

This memory verse is one of my personal favorites. Study it carefully; it only lists three requirements of God for man. The last one, humility, is the most difficult for man. We tend in our flesh – our old sin nature, to not want to be humble. Doing justly, is obeying Jesus' Golden Rule – treating everyone justly, like we want them to treat us. To love mercy means to be merciful in our dealings with others. This is equivalent to Jesus' second commandment to love our neighbor. Study it, this short Scripture is a pocket edition of the Decalogue given to Moses.

Nahum 1:7 – *The Lord is good, A strong hold in the day of trouble: and He knoweth them that trust in Him.*

This little gem is a nugget of strength when we face great peril. It requires faith for us to trust, and we get the needed faith from the same One we must trust. When we face circumstances where all is lost, it is well for us to know our soul and spirit are safe with the Lord.

Habakkuk 3:18 - *Yet I will rejoice in the Lord, I will joy in the God of my salvation.*

This bit of poetry here is reminiscent of some of the writings of David or Solomon. These old time ministers were quite vocal in their praise of their Savior – we could learn from them.

Zephaniah 3:17 – *The Lord thy God in the midst of thee is mighty; He will save, He will rejoice over thee with joy; He will rest in His love, He will joy over thee with singing.*

Another bit of prose styled in the manner of King David and his son, King Solomon. This verse here hints to us of a very close walk with God on the part of the author. He has experienced the love of the Lord and is paying praise to Him for it.

Haggai 1:7 – *Thus sayeth the Lord of hosts; consider your ways.*

This is telling us to plan and do all our works in a responsible manner. God is a God of order who expects us to also consider our actions.

Zechariah 2:10 – *Sing and rejoice, O daughter of Zion: for, lo, I come, and I will dwell in the midst of thee, saith the Lord.*

Zechariah was measuring the city of Jerusalem here and was paying homage to the Lord for his work. Here and elsewhere in God's Word we are told to do our best in whatever we are doing since all honorable work is to be done as unto the Lord and not just unto, (to please) the boss.

Malachi 3:10 – *Bring ye the all the tithes into the storehouse, that there may be meat in mine house, and prove me now herewith, saith the Lord of hosts, if I will not open you the windows of heaven, and pour you out a blessing, that there shall not be room enough to receive it.*

This is a favorite passage for the pastor to hit on sometimes, just before the plate is passed. It is a solemn vow from God to return blessings to those who cheerfully give. It has been displayed and proven for centuries, yet man is reluctant to accept God's promise.

Matthew 1:18-25 – *Now the birth of Jesus Christ was on this wise: When as His mother Mary was espoused to Joseph, before they came together, she was found with child of the Holy Ghost. 19 – Then Joseph her husband, being a just man, and not willing to make her a public example, was minded to put her away privily. 20 – But while he thought on these things, behold, the angel of the Lord appeared unto him in a dream, saying, Joseph, thou son of David, fear not to take unto thee Mary thou wife; for that which is conceived in her is of the Holy Ghost. 21 – And she shall bring forth a son, and thou shall call his name Jesus: for He shall save His people from their sins. 22 – Now all this was done, that it might be fulfilled which was spoken of the Lord by the prophet, saying, 23 – Behold, a virgin shall be with child, and shall bring forth a son, and they shall call his name Emanuel, which being interpreted is, God with us. 24 – Then Joseph being raised from sleep did as the angel of the Lord had bidden him, and took unto himself his wife: 25 – And knew her not till she had brought her firstborn son: and he called his name Jesus.*

This account of the events just prior to the birth of Jesus Christ is one of the most tender passages in the Bible. I count among my most memorable experiences the listening to Shirley reciting this rather long passage of memory verse Scripture. When she had it well memorized, it took/takes her three breaths to complete in about a minute's delivery time. Joseph exhibited strong faith and exemplary self-control to accomplish the things recounted here. God chose both Mary and Joseph for their unique roles in the birth of our Savior. He then gave them assurances through His angel, by his appearing to them and instructing them in what God expected of them. Perhaps we will be given a chance to personally thank them across Jordan – I expect we will see a long line of other well-wishers there.

Matthew 5:14-19 – *Ye are the light of the world. A city that is set on an hill cannot be hid. 15 – Neither do men light a candle, and put it under a bushel, but on a candlestick; and it giveth light unto all that are in the house. 16 – Let your light so shine before men, that they may see your good works, and glorify your Father which is in heaven. 17 – Think not that I am come to destroy the law, or the prophets: I am not come to destroy, but to fulfill. 18 – For verily I say unto you, till heaven and earth pass, one jot or one tittle shall in no wise pass from the law, till all be fulfilled. 19 – Whosoever therefore shall break one of these least commandments, and shall teach men so, he shall be called the least in the kingdom of heaven: but whosoever shall do and teach them, the same shall be called great in the kingdom of heaven.*

These memory verses cover quiet a bit of area. This is addressed to followers of Christ, and commissions them as light bearers for Him and His cause. We serve Him as ambassadors of light in a foreign land – this lost, darkened, and sinful world. More of the message is about not restricting the light we make available to others by putting it under a basket, but to set it high in our life's structure so it is effective to many who struggle in the darkness of sin. Then we are told that Jesus didn't come here as a man to destroy His Father's laws, rules nor commandments. We should remember this when anyone (it matters not a whit how many degrees of higher learning they claim) tells us that certain things from Old Testament times have been "done away with." Among these things are healing, speaking in tongues, keeping the Sabbath – (Saturday), prophesy, dream revelation, direct words from the Lord, Holy Spirit direction, words of Holy wisdom from a "Nathan," God's judgments on nations and individuals, angels, anointing, fasting – and the list goes on as men strive to institute their reasoning as replacements for those so called "Old Testament" practices and events. If Jesus Christ didn't cancel these *laws and the prophets* important to the Father, who could? The pope can't, even if he claims to be able to, not the Southern Baptist Convention, the President, Supreme Court nor any other earthly entity. It is notable that the misguided cannot destroy God's kingdom assets, they can still be forgiven their mischief and attain passage to heaven – where they will be demoted in status to the least among the heavenly host.

Matthew 6:9-34 – *After this manner therefore pray ye: our Father which art in heaven, hallowed be thy name. 10 – Thy kingdom come. Thy will be done in earth, as it is in heaven. 11 – Give us this day our daily bread. 12 – And forgive us our debts, as we forgive our debtors. 13 – And lead us not into temptation, but deliver us from evil: for thine is the kingdom, and the power, and the glory, for ever. Amen. 14 – For if ye forgive men their trespasses, your heavenly Father will also forgive you: 15 - But if you forgive not men their trespasses, neither will your Father forgive your trespasses. 16 – Moreover when ye fast, be not, as the hypocrites, of a sad countenance: for they disfigure their faces, that they may appear unto men to fast. Verily I say unto you, they have their reward. 17 – But thou, when thou fasteth, anoint thine head, and wash thy face; 18 – That thou appear not unto men to fast, but unto thy Father which is in secret: and thy Father, which seeth in secret, shall reward thee openly. 19 - Lay not up for yourselves treasures upon earth, where moth and rust doth corrupt, and where thieves break through and steal: 20 – But lay up for yourselves treasures in heaven, where neither moth nor rust doth corrupt, and where thieves do not break through nor steal: 21 – For where your treasure is, there will your heart be also. 22 – The light of the body is the eye: if therefore thine eye be single, thy whole body shall be full of light. 23 – But if thine eye be evil, thy whole body shall be full of darkness. If therefore the light that is in thee be darkness, how great is that darkness! 24 – No man can serve two masters: for either he will hate the one, and love the other; or else he will hold to the one, and despise the other. Ye cannot serve God and mammon. 25 – Therefore I say unto you, take no thought for your life, what ye shall eat, or what ye shall drink; nor yet for your body, what ye shall put on. Is not the life more than meat, and the body than raiment? 26 – Behold the fowls of the air: for they sow not, neither do they reap, nor gather into barns; yet your heavenly Father feedeth them. Are ye not much better than they? 27 – Which of you by taking thought can add one cubit unto his stature? 28 – And why take ye thought for raiment? Consider the lilies of the field, how they grow; they toil not, neither do they spin: 29 -And yet I say unto you, that even Solomon in all his glory was not arrayed like one of these. 30 – Wherefore, if God so clothe the grass of the field, which today is, and tomorrow is cast into the oven, shall He not much more clothe you, O ye of little faith? 31 – Therefore take no thought, saying, what shall we eat? Or, what shall we drink? or, wherewithal shall we be clothed? 32 – (for after all these things do the Gentiles seek:) for your heavenly Father knoweth that ye have need of all these things. 33 – But seek ye first the kingdom of God, and His righteousness; and all these things shall be added unto you. 34 – Take therefore no thought for the morrow: for the morrow shall take thought for the things of itself. Sufficient unto the day is the evil thereof.*

This longest of our memory Scriptures starts with what is called the Lord's prayer (verses 9-15) and continues to explore many other things Jesus wanted to share with us. Let's look at some of those things now. Right away we see we are to pray aloud in groups at times since He starts His model prayer with **our** Father. I recall discussing this with my earthly father when he was about ninety years old, and we were discussing the matter of public prayer. This first sentence also settles for anyone who has a question concerning just exactly where God the Father makes His abode. The sentence's conclusion reminds us that the name of our Creator is to be revered above every name. The second sentence reminds us that His kingdom is coming soon and that His will in our lives and everything else is mandated to be followed both here on this earth and also in heaven, which seem from this, to be separate localities. We then see that we are to look to Him for our food and necessities of life as well as forgiveness; and that His forgiveness is dependent upon our exercise of the same toward others. At verse 13 God is never our tempter (which tells who is, since there are only two spiritual forces) but that He delivers us from the powers of Satan. It concludes saying truthfully that God owns His kingdom, is all powerful, throughout eternity – FOREVER. This verse here concludes with the prayerful ending of Amen; one of the few such examples in the Bible, and identifying the preceding verses as a prayer ... a model prayer for us to emulate. The next verse somewhat repeats verse 12 amplifying the two-way relationship in forgiveness. At 16 we see Jesus giving explicit instructions concerning fasting. The general idea is to not be wearing your sack cloth and ashes and moaning and murmuring about great sacrifices. This applies to good works too, as shown elsewhere. The reference to "they have their reward" is talking to the fact that the braggart/murmurer gets a short-lived prideful ego-boost grandstanding his sham piety, while the one who follows Christ's instructions will receive a heavenly reward for eternity. The show-off gets his ego stroked, but the obeyer is rewarded openly by the Father, so he reaps two rewards. At 19 we are told to not be stashing away treasures here and now, but to send things dear to our hearts ahead to heaven where they will be kept safely and securely. One way to send your treasures ahead is take some money and/or effort to help some needy people, visit some shut-in or nursing home person, or any unselfish thing for others. You will get a good feeling in your heart now and have rewards in heaven awaiting your arrival at the mansion He has prepared for you. We then see that the human eye reflects much information to those around who care to observe. A well trained investigator/interrogator knows to watch the eyes of a suspect when questioning. A very successful polygraph operator told me he could usually tell when a response was untruthful from the eye's reaction before the machine's ink needles could indicate it. At memory verse 24 we see that great truth stating no one can serve two masters. We see well educated religious leaders who think this is not true. The people following Rick Warren in his ill-fated "Chrislam" heresy should consider what Jesus said here. Anyone who thinks they can love money and love God and their neighbor are in grave danger of following the broad way which leads to destruction. The concluding verses are a broad indictment against the hedonistic me-myself-and-I culture we are inundated in today. The things He tells us to not be overly concerned with in life are the exact things modern society busies themselves with constantly. The *Wall Street Journal* publishes a slick magazine supplement with their Saturday edition that highlights the very things Jesus told us to not waste our time and resources on. It appears to me that Satan has a list of things for man to covet that reverse-mirrors the things Jesus spoke of here. We are told to seek kingdom things and practices and all the desires of our hearts will be supplied. Reviewing these Scriptures, I was reminded by a note attached to the sheet having these memory verses displayed. The note is a hand-written one, where my bilingual good friend, Gene Petitt, wrote the words and phonetic clues for the Lord's Prayer in Spanish about twenty years ago. I was able to get about half of it down good enough to recite it, but over the years I only recite the first verse sometimes when I am with Spanish speakers saying prayers. I will start my prayer with the introductory words in Spanish, then revert to English to conclude; those few words are: *Padre nuestro que estas en los cielos, sanctificado sea tu nombre.* Thank God, He knows what we are saying to Him in any language or just in our minds and hearts. We can fool one another, perhaps even the man with the box, but our Creator sees on the heart of man!

Matthew 7:1-27 – *Judge not, that ye be not judged. 2 – For with what judgment ye judge, ye shall be judged: and with what measure ye mete, it shall be measured to you again.*

This seems to the best known verse in the Bible to some people, the people who live lifestyles that are in direct opposition to the other things proscribed elsewhere in God's word. Even the pope recently said "Who am I to Judge?" when asked about homosexuality. No human needs to judge that sinful practice as God has already done so. There's a big difference in judging and quoting or citing a previous judgment by God. The secular crowd has a pithy saying demonstrating the message of verse 2; they say, "What goes around comes around." If they knew this agrees with the Bible they would likely drop it from their lexicon. 3-4-5 – *And why beholdest thou the mote in thy brother's eye, but considerest not the beam in thine own eye?* Here we can help our understanding a mite by examining what is meant by "mote" and "beam." A mote is a speck, a dot, something very small, while the beam mentioned here means a large wood board or plank. Think of a particle of sawdust and a 4X8 building roof support. The inference here is to us ignoring our big gaffes and mistakes while calling attention to small infractions on the part of others. Think of the obese glutton criticizing some petite person helping themselves to a second piece of pie. 4 – *Or how wilt thou say to thy brother, let me pull out the mote out of thine eye; and, behold, a beam is in thine own eye? 5 – Thou hypocrite, first cast out the beam out of thine own eye; and then shalt thou see clearly to cast out the mote out of thy brother's eye. 6 – Give not that which is holy unto the dogs, neither cast ye your pearls before swine, lest they trample them under their feet, and turn again and rend you.* This is something we can fall into easily while attempting to be helpful. Trying to talk sense to an inebriated person, attempting to witness to someone high on dope are examples. You must wait until they are in their right mind to be effective. Someone interrupting a speaker with jeers and taunting is another real life example. Such distraction must be overcome by ignoring the source of trouble or gently removing them. 7-8 – *Ask, and it shall be given you; seek, and ye shall find; knock, and it shall be opened unto you: For everyone that asketh receiveth; and he that seeketh findeth; and to him that knocketh it shall be opened.* This is Jesus' promise to answer our requests that are in accordance with His will. So many times we see these principles validated. Upon occasion He fails to fulfill our earnest plea, only to give us something better for us, in His perfect timing. If you have never experienced this, may I suggest you start paying more attention, don't murmur, and be more thankful for the good gifts you receive from His strong stretched out arm. 9 and 10 – *Or what man is there of you, whom if his son ask bread, will he give him a stone? Or if he ask a fish, will he give him a serpent?* These unseemly suggestions were made in the form of questions to score the point that no normal father would mistreat his son in such manner. 7:11 – *If ye then, being evil, know how to give good gifts unto your children, how much more shall your Father which is in heaven give good things to them that ask Him?* This is an easily grasped lesson comparing men's actions with their children with the treatment we can rightfully expect from our heavenly Father. 12 – *Therefore all things whatsoever ye would that men should do to you, do ye even so to them: for this is the law and the prophets.* Did everyone catch that? That is the Golden Rule given here by Jesus Christ as a universal rule that, if followed, promises peace and tranquility for everyone, everywhere. If nations practiced this simple, easy to understand rule, we would have had thousands less wars since Jesus first uttered the famous words. 13-14 – *Enter ye in at the strait gate: for wide is the gate, and broad is the way, that leadeth to destruction, and many there be which go in thereat: Because strait is the gate, and narrow is the way, which leadeth unto life, and few there be that find it.* Most human beings are programmed to usually take the "easy way out" when making decisions. This Scripture encourages us to make the required extra effort in making good choices and eschew the easy ways in life while obeying our consciences and take the narrow way to eventual rewards in heaven. People, who go through life opting always for the easy way waste life's most precious assets. They drink in bars and eat in food lines. They live in godless, shacking up arrangements, abort their babies, live hand-to-mouth and pay no taxes. They spend much of their lives in jails and prisons, don't even try to keep a job, but live on the government dole. They live apart from their family, blame others for their troubles, die alone in the emergency room or flop house. The county buries their body and Satan takes their soul! That is the easy way. Those of us who have been saved from destruction and are laboring to keep on the strait (narrow) way have an obligation to tell those people that there is a much better way to live. We need to love those people and show them there is a better lifestyle, and live an example before them. With all of this said, the closing sentence here announces the sad truth that few in our society ever find their narrow gate to eternal bliss in heaven. 15-20 – *Beware of false prophets, which come to you in sheep's clothing, but inwardly they are ravening wolves. 16 – Ye shall know them by their fruits. Do men gather grapes of thorns, or figs of thistles? 17 – Even so every good tree bringeth forth good fruit; but a corrupt tree bringeth forth evil fruit. 18 – A good tree cannot bring forth evil fruit, neither can a corrupt tree bring forth good fruit.*

19 – Every tree that bringeth not forth good fruit is hewn down, and cast into the fire. 20 – Wherefore by their fruits shall ye know them.

This is the way we can winnow people using the strong east wind of God's truth and discern which sheep in the flock are really wolves among us to do harm to the congregation. Don't look on their outward appearance as we recently read. Since we cannot see into their hearts, we should follow His instructions, and check their fruit basket. The fruits alluded to here are the fruits of the Spirit Paul listed for us at Galatians 5:22-23. It doesn't matter who they are; Sunday school teacher, president of the biggest bank in town, song leader or pastor, if they don't show the fruits, we need to see them converted or moved outside. If you find yourself in a church run by these kinds of people, remove yourself … pronto! *21-23 – Not everyone that saith unto me, Lord, Lord, shall enter into the kingdom of heaven; but he that doeth the will of my father which is in heaven. 22 – Many will say to me in that day, Lord, Lord, have we not prophesied in thy name? And in thy name have cast out devils? And in thy name done many wonderful works? 23 – And then will I profess unto them, I never knew you: depart from me, ye that work inequity.*

These memory verses here are an example of the several Scriptures which may lead to the assumption that there are few in today's churches who are truly saved. If people are casting out devils, but Jesus says He doesn't even know them, who can we think to be born again and saved? Answer: Those who display the fruit mentioned earlier. Let us not rely on our supposed good works to save our souls. Let us accept Jesus' offer of salvation and see to our fruit production, not our speaking in tongues, and supporting missions. If we know <u>of</u> God He knows <u>of</u> us, but if you <u>know</u> Him then He <u>knows</u> you.

Matthew 7:24-27 – *Therefore whosoever heareth these sayimgs of mine, and doeth them, I will liken him unto a wise man, which built his house upon a rock: 25 – And the rain descended, and the floods came, and the winds blew, and beat upon that house; and it fell not; for it was founded upon a rock. 26- And every one that heareth these sayings of mine, and doeth them not, shall be likened unto a foolish man, which built his house upon the sand: 27 – And the rain descended, and the floods came, and the winds blew, and beat upon that house; and it fell: and great was the fall of it.*

This memory Scripture is a vivid word-picture describing the difference between those who heed Christ's warnings and those who ignore them. In our time just about everyone has heard the teachings of Jesus Christ, but the majority of them pay little or no heed to them. The shifting sands that the world's various religions are based on do not compare with the bedrock of Christianity.

Matthew 10:29-33 – *Are not two sparrows sold for a farthing? And one of them shall not fall on the ground without your Father. 30 – But the very hairs of your head are all numbered. 31 – Fear ye not therefore, ye are of more value than many sparrows. 32 – Whosoever therefore shall confess me before men, him will I confess also before my Father which is in heaven. 33 – But whosoever shall deny me before men, him will I also deny before my Father which is in heaven.*

The great truth taught here by Jesus is that all-knowing God knows the very most minute details of His creation. Some people think this is an over statement on the part of Jesus, said for effect. I don't think Jesus was spoofing in His statement. I believe He was speaking truth, and I accept it as that. If we compare the astronomical vastness and incredible intricacies of His universe and the unimaginable construction of the human body, counting the few thousand hairs on a few billion heads is a snap. A few years ago I was visiting my old and dear friend, Phil, after his daughter, Pat, had called saying that Hospice had called the Priest who had administered final rites. She spoke as if it were only a matter of hours, saying if I wanted to see him before he passed away, I should come now. I dropped everything, flew the hundred miles to San Angelo, and was at his bedside in under an hour. In trying to console Phil I assured him God was in control, and even knew the number of hairs on our heads. At this he became more alert and demanded "Who told you that?" When I said it's in the Bible, he wanted to see it. The Holy Spirit surely guided my efforts, because I was able to accommodate him a few minutes later. This revelation energized Phil greatly, leading to a long conversation leading to a discussion concerning our salvation. Later Phil talked to his priest regarding this, and he lived for over a year ..., a year blessed with a clearer understanding of God's truths.

Matthew 11:28-30 — *Come unto me, all ye that labour and are heavy laden, and I will give you rest. 29 – Take my yoke upon you, and learn of me; for I am meek and lowly in heart: and ye shall find rest unto your souls. 30 – For my yoke is easy, and my burden is light.*

Whenever we catch ourselves murmuring and complaining about the many heavy burdens we have because we are Christians and struggling to keep His commandments, we should stop and think. Think, who are we doing this for, is it for Him or us, or maybe the devil through pride? If we say being a Christian is sooo difficult, we are contradicting Jesus' words here. Think about it! Then we should repent for abetting Satan and take up our cross – it is very light compared to the one He carried up Calvary's hill for our salvation.

Matthew 18:18-20 — *Verily I say unto you, whatsoever ye shall bind on earth shall be bound in heaven: and whatsoever ye shall loose on earth shall be loosed in heaven. 19 – Again I say unto you, that if two of you shall agree on earth as touching any thing that they shall ask, it shall be done for them of my Father which is in heaven. 20 – For where two or three are gathered together in my name, there am I in the midst of them.*

These words from our Savior are among the strongest affirmations in the whole Bible. What a great blessing to be assured by the One who can do anything – **anything,** to tell us He hears our supplications and stands ready to fulfill our needs. We only expect His deliverance of those things which He knows are for our good ... remember – a good father will not give His son a serpent. When we gather with other believers in His presence we represent a powerful voting bloc.

Matthew 22:37-40 — *Jesus said unto him, thou shall love the Lord thy God with all thy heart, and with all thy soul, and with all thy mind. 38 – This is the first and great commandment. 39 – And the second is like unto it, thou shalt love thy neighbor as thyself. 40 – On these two commandments hang all the law and the prophets.*

This is a key Scripture in the Bible. These two commandments of Christ do NOT replace any of the ten which God gave to Moses for His people. These two here rather confirm all of the ten. Some "feel good, prosperity" preachers teach the second commandment given here directs us to love ourselves. That is false teaching - Satan takes care of that department for all of us.

Matthew 28:18-20 – *And Jesus came and spake unto them, saying, all power is given unto me in heaven and in earth. 19 – Go ye therefore, and teach all nations, baptizing them in the name of the Father, and of the Son, and of the Holy Ghost: 20 – Teaching them to observe all things whatsoever I have commanded you: And, lo, I am with you alway, even unto the end of the world. Amen.*

These memory verses contain the "Great Commission" where Jesus mandated the sending forth of missionaries all over the face of the earth to bring the Gospel, the good news, to people who haven't had His message of salvation before. This, of course includes the sending of Bibles to those people, printed in their native language. New Tribes Missions in Sanford, Florida sends missionaries to remote locations to learn the natives' language and establish an alphabet to allow those people to have the Bible in their working language. Wycliff translators worked in this area for many years. Sadly, Wycliff recently agreed to alter God's Word to accommodate Islam's teaching that Jesus Christ was/is not Deity. We need to remember the warnings in Revelation against adding to or subtracting from His word. Gilbertex Foundation, Inc. which holds all rights to this book in your hands sends Bibles each month through the good efforts of the American Bible Society, to selected countries. By purchasing this book, people help observe the Great Commission through the efforts of those on the front lines – our missionary friends. The closing sentence is Jesus' vow to be with us in these efforts, *even unto the end of the world.* No higher calling exists this side of Jordan.

Mark 8:31-33 – *And He began to teach them, that the son of man must suffer many things, and be rejected of the elders, and of the chief priests, and scribes, and be killed, and after three days rise again. 32 – And He spake that saying openly. And Peter took Him, and began to rebuke Him. 33 – But when He had turned about and looked on His disciples, He rebuked Peter, saying, Get thee behind me, Satan: for thou savourest not the things that be of God, but the things that be of men.*

This Scripture is one of the saddest in the Bible, I think. Jesus is trying to prepare His disciples for the coming events – the events for which His life here on earth was lived. Peter didn't want to hear it, and subsequent events show the others didn't really comprehend what Jesus was trying to tell them. We have preachers and others today trying to prepare our people for the soon to be rapture of God's people from the earth, and many are like Peter – in denial; or like the others, uncomprehending.

Mark 8:36-38 – *For what shall it profit a man, if he shall gain the whole world, and lose his own soul? 37 – Or what shall a man give in exchange for his soul? 38 – Whosoever therefore shall be ashamed of me and of my words in this adulterous and sinful generation; of him also shall the son of man be ashamed, when he cometh in the glory of his Father with the holy angels.*

What a strong Scripture these three memory verses are! Does that first one remind us of any of today's big shots? We see them amassing money-power-prestige-acclaim, as if they think it will last forever. Reminds one of Esau who traded his future inheritance for a bowl of red beans and some cornbread. The next two verses examine the fate of those who are ashamed of the world's Savior. We see leaders today, who will not call the name of Jesus in a public forum. A president, who ordered His crosses covered from camera view before speaking at a Christian university. That university dean and other officials missed an excellent opportunity by not just canceling the little man's appearance!

Mark 10:14-15 – *But when Jesus saw it, He was much displeased, and said unto them, suffer the little children to come unto me, and forbid them not; for of such is the kingdom of God. 15 – Verily I say unto you, whosoever shall not receive the kingdom of God as a little child, he shall not enter therein.*

This memory verse teaches several different but connected lessons. The disciples had tried to get the little ones to go play outside or some such, so the grown-ups could visit. We see here one of the few times where the Bible mentions Jesus being displeased. His reaction was openly stated for everyone, including the kids, to hear these adults being reprimanded for their actions. Jesus said the kingdom of God is made up of children and older folk, who came to Him as children. Wonder what He will have to say to our women's libbers and those nine robes about the countless millions of very littlest children we have sacrificed on the Molech altar of selfishness?

Mark 10:43-45 – *But so shall it not be among you: but whosoever will be great among you, shall be your minister: 44 – And whosoever of you will be the chiefest, shall be servant of all. 45 – For even the son of man came not to be ministered unto, but to minister, and to give his life a ransom for many.*

These words from Christ were spoken openly and earnestly to teach his disciples some humility and sense of order. He explained again that He was going to die for the "ransom" - salvation of many. That many has proven to be millions since He uttered those prophetic truths. Sadly, while those millions of saints have gone on to their mansions in heaven, billions have taken the broad way to hell.

Luke 1:30-35 – *And the angel said unto her, fear not, Mary: for thou hast found favour with God. 31 – And, behold, thou shalt conceive in thy womb, and bring forth a son, and shalt call His name Jesus. 32 – He shall be great, and shall be called the son of the Highest: and the Lord God shall give unto Him the throne of His Father David: 33 – And He shall reign over the house of Jacob for ever; and of His kingdom there shall be no end. 34 – Then said Mary unto the angel, How shall this be, seeing I know not a man? 35 – And the angel answered and said unto her, the Holy Ghost shall come upon thee, and the power of the Highest shall overshadow thee: therefore also that holy thing which shall be born of thee shall be called the son of God.*

There we have it, the physician, Dr. Luke reports the angel's pronouncement in the very most non-medical terms. For her to accept the words of the angel, required Mary to have much faith. When we are faced with hard-to-accept directions from God, we must rely on Him to give us the faith to accept His truths. We don't need to struggle with it or fight against it – only accept it.

Luke 2:1-20 – *And it came to pass in those days, that there went out a decree from Caesar Augustus, that all the world should be taxed. 2 - (and this taxing was first made when Cyrenius was governor of Syria.) 3 – And all went to be taxed, every one into his own city. 4 – And Joseph also went up from Galilee, out of the city of Nazareth, into Judaea, unto the city of David, which is called Bethlehem; (because he was of the house and lineage of David:) 5 – To be taxed with Mary his espoused wife, being great with child. 6 – And so it was, that, while they were there, the days were accomplished that she should be delivered. 7 – And she brought forth her firstborn son, and wrapped him in swaddling clothes, and laid him in a manger; because there was no room for them in the inn. 8 – And there were in the same country shepherds abiding in the field, keeping watch over their flock by night. 9 - and, lo, the angel of the Lord came upon them, and the glory of the Lord shone round about them: and they were sore afraid. 10 – And the angel said unto them, fear not: for, behold, I bring you good tidings of great joy, which shall be to all people. 11 – For unto you is born this day in the city of David a Saviour, which is Christ the Lord. 12 – And this shall be a sign unto you; ye shall find the babe wrapped in swaddling clothes, lying in a manger. 13 – And suddenly there was with the angel a multitude of the heavenly host praising God, and saying, 14 – Glory to God in the highest, and on earth peace, good will toward men. 15 – And it came to pass, as the angels were gone away from them into heaven, the shepherds said one to another, let us now go even unto Bethlehem, and see this thing which is come to pass, which the Lord has made known unto us. 16 – And they came with haste, and found Mary, and Joseph, and the babe lying in a manger. 17 – And when they had seen it, they made known abroad the saying which was told them concerning this child. 18 – And all they that heard it wondered at those things which were told them by the shepherds. 19 – But Mary kept all these things, and pondered them in her heart. 20 – And the shepherds returned, glorifying and praising God for all the things that they had heard and seen, as it was told unto them.*

There it is, as recorded and translated into the beautiful prose and poetry of the KJV Bible. This account of the birth of the baby Jesus is replete with several sub-messages. It becomes even more informative with each rereading. By the time it has been committed to memory it becomes a small book of interesting details. Joseph and Mary were returning to their home town to be included in the census and pay their taxes. It was needed that she be there, too, in order to prevent additional levy and more official paper work. We can easily imagine her midwife didn't approve of Mary riding a donkey all that distance in her ninth month. Matthew and John recount the birth of Jesus. Mark begins his recounting of the Savior's life at the river Jordan, where John the Baptist was baptizing Jesus. This account here from the pen of Dr. Luke is the longest of the three, but we chose it to memorize because of its detail and scope. Read them all, they have different viewpoints, but all agree in substance.

Luke 5:39 – *No man also having drunk old wine straightway desireth new: for he saith, the old is better.*

This memory verse is the concluding line for the 5th chapter of the book of Luke. These are the words of Jesus Christ and the context is the discussion of the practice of putting new wine into new bottles rather than in older, weaker bottles. The pressures generated from the fermentation of newly produced wine requires strong bottles. Jesus could be considered an expert in such matters in his humanity, since He converted over a hundred gallons of cistern water into wine – very good wine, at the wedding celebration at Cana, as recorded in John's Gospel. This account here in Luke tells several truths. He is speaking of wine, not Welch's grape juice nor Kool-Aid. With no refrigeration nor pasteurization available, grape juice will revert to wine or vinegar rather quickly.

Luke 9:23 – *And He said to them all, if any man will come after me, let him deny himself, and take up his cross daily, and follow me.*

This is the memory verse assigned in the first lesson of the Masterlife class I mentioned in the first of the book. The cross Jesus is referencing here is the works the Lord has given to each of His followers. We all have assignments in our earthly life. There are different jobs for people with different gifts.

Luke 14:26-27 - *If any man come to me, and hate not his father, and mother, and wife, and children, and brethren, and sisters, yea, and his own life also, he cannot be my disciple. 27 – And whosoever doth not bear his cross, and come after me, he cannot be my disciple.*

If this were the only quote from Jesus in the Bible we would have a different picture of Him and His teachings. Many times He instructs on the value of love among people. Several historic and contemporary commentators agree that He is saying here that we must not love family and ourselves more than we do Him and His kingdom. We see again here the importance of taking up our cross and following His lead.

Luke 14:33 – *So likewise, whosoever he be of you that foresaketh not all that he hath, he cannot be my disciple.*

If your golf score, them cowboys, your education, family, business, *or anything else* is more important to you than His work, you aren't on His team. A person can be heaven bound, based on His redeeming grace encumbered with baggage, but not be His disciple, I think.

John 1:1-14 – *In the beginning was the Word, and the Word was with God, and the Word was God. 2 – The same was in the beginning with God. 3 – All things were made by Him; and without Him was not anything made that was made. 4 – In Him was life; and the life was the light of men. 5 – And the light shineth in darkness; and the darkness comprehended it not. 6 – There was a man sent from God, whose name was John. 7 – The same came for a witness, to bear witness of the Light, that all men through him might believe. 8 – He was not that Light, but was sent to bear witness of that Light. 9 – That was the true Light, which lighteth every man that cometh into the world. 10 - He was in the world, and the world was made by Him, and the world knew Him not. 11 – He came unto His own, and His own received Him not. 12 – But as many as received Him, to them gave He power to become the sons of God, even to them that believe on His name: 13 – Which were born, not of blood, nor of will of the flesh, nor of will of man, but of God. 14 – And the word was made flesh, and dwelt among us, (and we beheld His glory, the glory as of the only begotten of the father,) full of grace and truth.*

Reading the Genesis account, one might assume God the Father was the One who created everything. This Scripture sheds additional light on the matter. This is another thing we may only understand partly as peering through a glass darkly. The calling Christ the Word is a little confusing at first, but it becomes abundantly clear that is what is happening here. Of course many other positive things are equated with Him throughout the Bible.

John 3:3 — Jesus answered and said unto him, verily, verily, I say unto thee, Except a man be born again, he cannot see the kingdom of God.

This important memory verse is an accounting of a discussion between Jesus and Nicodemus, an educated Jewish leader who came late in the evening to learn from Jesus. Here Jesus makes it very clear that a person must undergo a major change from their sinful life and become a new man spiritually in order to go to heaven when they pass from this earthly life. It is clear that people, who think being baptized into some church affiliation is salvation are deluded. Likewise, someone who thinks they have been a Christian "all my life" hasn't a clue about the truth spoken by Jesus Christ here.

John 3:14-21 — *And as Moses lifted up the serpent in the wilderness, even so must the Son of man be lifted up: 15 — That whosoever believeth in Him should not perish, but have eternal life. 16 — For God so loved the world, that He gave His only begotten Son, that whosoever believeth in Him should not perish, but have everlasting life. 17 — For God sent not His Son into the world to condemn the world; but that the world through Him might be saved. 18 — He that believeth on Him is not condemned: but he that believeth not is condemned already, because he hath not believed in the name of the only begotten Son of God. 19 — And this is the condemnation, that light is come into the world, and men loved darkness rather than light, because their deeds were evil. 20 — For everyone that doeth evil hateth the light, neither cometh to the light, lest his deeds should be reproved. 21 — But he that doeth truth cometh to the light, that his deeds may be made manifest, that they are wrought in God.*

Things haven't changed much since these words of truth were taught by Jesus. Evil men set on doing evil deeds still prefer the darkness to ply their nefarious trade. Crime and sinfulness increase everywhere as the hours of darkness come on. Contained in this memory Scripture is the most familiar verse in the New Testament – John 3:16, this verse is the heart of the Gospel of Jesus Christ.

John 4:35-36 – *Say not ye, there are yet four months, and then cometh harvest? Behold, I say unto you, lift up your eyes, and look on the fields; for they are white already to harvest. 36 – And he that reapeth receiveth wages, and gathereth fruit unto life eternal: that both he that soweth and he that reapeth may rejoice together.*

Most of the people inhabiting the places Jesus trod were fishermen, sheep and cattle people and agriculture workers. I happened to be born into a family of farmers who had some cattle and sheep etc. To me, the reference here to fields white unto harvest reminds me of the cotton fields of my youth. After first frost, freezing nights, the cotton fields were, indeed, as white as snow and ready for harvest. Today we live in perilous times with much persecution of God's people by powers in high places, but we also have great opportunities for harvest of precious souls in fields ripe for harvest. Let us be about our Father's business!

John 5:19 – *Then answered Jesus and said unto them, verily, verily, I say unto you, the Son can do nothing of himself, but what he seeth the Father do: for what things soever he doeth, these also doeth the son likewise.*

I recall this particular memory verse was very difficult for me, as the language is somewhat contorted while delivering the intended message right on target. I think those things we learned at our parent's side are the most natural and easy to learn of all life's lessons. Godly parents are a great blessing for any child.

John 6:35 – *And Jesus said unto them, I am the bread of life: he that cometh to me shall never hunger; and he that believeth on on me shall never thirst.*

Reading this memory verse here in context shows Jesus was speaking of spiritual things. He was discussing men's need for salvation. However, looking back fondly at my own life of well over four score years, I have never suffered from need for bread nor water. Born and raised my early years during the great depression and World War II in a good, but poor Christian family, I have never suffered for want of any need.

John 8:31-32 – *Then said Jesus to those Jews which believed on Him, If ye continue in my word, then are ye my disciples indeed; 32 – and ye shall know the truth, and the truth shall make you free.*

This is a basic, bedrock truth told by Jesus to His believing countrymen. It is still true today to Jews and Gentiles alike. His people can learn more of Him by staying in the Word. He stands ready always to reveal more of His truth to us always. His vow to use His truth to make us free – free in Him, is a timeless promise to us.

John 8:47 – *He that is of God heareth God's words: ye therefore hear them not, because ye are not of God.*

This memory verse comes to us from a discussion Jesus had with the Jewish leaders, who persecuted Him. He has just told them that they were being influenced by the devil to not believe the truths Jesus was teaching. Jesus had just told them that the devil was/is the father of lies and a murderer from the start. We, today, have Jesus' truth available in the Bible and through prayer. The comforter He sent (the Holy Spirit) indwells each believer to lead us in truth. All we are called to do is believe on Him, who is the same yesterday, today and forever.

John 10:10 – *The thief cometh not, but for to steal, and to kill, and to destroy: I am come that they might have life, and that they might have it more abundantly.*

This easy to memorize verse contains a lot of truth in it. Sometimes the thief will resort to murder to prevent discovery of his stealing. Many times the thief destroys the crime scene in an attempt to cover his tracks. My family and I have been in the security field for well over half a century. Our professional dealings with thieves certainly validates Jesus' words here.

John 11:25 – *Jesus said unto her, I am the resurrection, and the life: he that believeth in me, though he were dead, yet shall he live:*

Jesus was speaking to Martha, whose brother Lazarus had recently died. Jesus had just told her that He was going to bring life back to Lazarus' body, and she misunderstood, thinking Jesus was speaking of Lazarus' soul in eternity. As Jesus told Martha here, He is the resurrection, the final redeemer of men's souls.

John 13:34-35 - *A new commandment I give unto you, That ye love one another; as I have loved you, that ye also love one another. 35 — By this shall all men know that ye are my disciples, if ye have love one to another.*

Christ had earlier told the twelve that they could recognize other believers by their displayed fruits of the spirit. Here He amplifies the earlier criterion, with this admonition to love one another. This standard of practice uniquely sets Christianity apart from the rest of human behavior, and is something we should cherish and delight in doing.

John 14:1-3 — *Let not your heart be troubled: ye believe in God, believe also in me. 2- In my Father's house are many mansions: if it were not so, I would have told you. I go to prepare a place for you. 3 — And if I go and prepare a place for you, I will come again, and receive you unto myself; that where I am, there ye may be also.*

These words from Jesus are a precious promise about what his adopted brothers and sisters can expect awaiting their arrival in heaven. When the devil is trying to cast doubt on you about heaven, this is a good memory verse to cast at him.

John 14:6 — *Jesus saith unto him, I am the way, the truth, and the life: no man cometh unto the Father, but by me.*

This is the Scripture to quote to those who claim there are many, diverse paths to salvation. There is much discussion among people claiming to be Christians about their claim. There is nothing in the Bible that buttresses their false claim. Only Jesus Christ can make this claim and produce the results. The pope, your pastor, nor the mechanic who fixes your car can help you here. It is the blood of Jesus, shed on Calvary's cross, and that alone, which allows us to come into the presence of Him and the Father.

John 14:21 – *He that hath my commandments, and keepeth them, he it is that loveth me: and he that loveth me shall be loved of my Father, and I will love him, and will manifest myself to him.*

We, today do not live under the law as those did in olden times, but Jesus shows us here that the keeping of His commandments is precious in His sight. The keeping of the commandments to love God with all our heart, mind, and soul, and loving others as we love ourselves, is how we can enjoy loving fellowship with our Savior and God.

John 14:23 – *Jesus answered and said unto him, if a man love me, he will keep my words: and my Father will love him, and we will come unto him, and make our abode with him.*

This memory verse reinforces the previous one and expands it also. Here we see the promise from Jesus that both He and the Father will make their abode, their home as it were, with us when we show our obedience by revering them by keeping their words.

John 15:5-13 – *I am the vine, ye are the branches: he that abideth in me, and I in him, the same bringeth forth much fruit: for without me ye can do nothing. 6 – If a man abide not in me, he is cast forth as a branch, and is withered; and men gather them, and cast them into the fire, and they are burned. 7 – If ye abide in me, and my words abide in you, ye shall ask what ye will, and it shall be done unto you. 8 – Herein is my Father glorified, that ye bear much fruit; so shall ye be my disciples. 9 – As the Father hath loved me, so have I loved you: continue ye in my love. 10- If ye keep my commandments, ye shall abide in my love; even as I have kept my Father's commandments, and abide in His love. 11 – These things have I spoken unto you, that my joy might remain in you, and that your joy might be full. 12 – This is my commandment, that ye love one another, as I have loved you. 13 – Greater love hath no man than this, that a man lay down his life for his friends.*

This soliloquy could be called Jesus' love fruit discourse. He begins by admonishing His followers to be fruitful while reminding us we are completely devoid of good works without Him. Then He reminds us of His other statements of how worthless dry branches are cast into the fire to be burned up. He tells us the Father is glorified when

His children *bear much fruit.* He could be referring to both children and fruits of the spirit. Throughout this Scripture the keeping of the commandments, love for one another, and the Father's love for His Son and us is stressed.

Acts 4:11-12 – *This is the stone which was set at naught of you builders, which is become the head of the corner. 12 – Neither is there salvation in any other: for there is none other name under heaven given among men, whereby we must be saved.*

Peter had preached to a large crowd regarding who Jesus Christ was and how the crowd, at the urging of their religious leaders, had demanded He be crucified. About five thousand had become converted, and this upset the Jewish leaders, who had Peter and his group held overnight to answer to the council the next day. Peter had restored health to a local cripple whom everyone knew. This had the council upset also. When they questioned Peter he gave Jesus Christ the credit for the good works and pointed out to them that they had rejected Jesus. We still see such injustices in the current times.

Romans 3:9-12 – *What then? Are we better than they? No, in no wise: for we have before proved both Jews and Gentiles, that they are all under sin; 10 – As it is written, there is none righteous, no, not one: 11 – There is none that understandeth, there is none that seeketh after God. 12 – They are all gone out of the way, they are together become unprofitable; there is none that doeth good, no, not one.*

Not a very pretty picture of mankind is it? Paul tells the people in the church at Rome that everyone – Jews and Gentiles alike are contemptible sinners. We don't like to see ourselves in the same light as our Creator sees us. The fact is, we cannot do <u>anything</u>, let alone anything good, apart from His enabling us.

Romans 3:23 – *For all have sinned, and come short of the glory of God;*

In case anyone missed the message earlier; here it is again. Paul is reminding us what the Holy Spirit is instructing him to reiterate; that natural man is a sinful creature, unable to correct his evil ways apart from the redeeming blood of Jesus.

Romans 5:8 – *But God commendeth His love toward us, in that, while we were yet sinners, Christ died for us.*

This short memory verse here continues Paul's earlier message about the utter depravity of sinful man, and man's dire need for Christ's sacrifice for man's redemption. Without our Creator's love for us we would have absolutely <u>no</u> hope.

Romans 6:12-14 – *Let not sin therefore reign in your mortal body, that ye should obey it in the lusts thereof. 13 – Neither yield ye your members as instruments of unrighteousness unto sin: but yield yourselves unto God, as those that are alive from the dead, and your members as instruments of righteousness unto God. 14 – For sin shall not have dominion over you: for ye are not under the law, but under grace.*

These three memory verses serve us well to remind us we live in the age of God's grace and forgiveness. We can see here that we are to constantly strive to deny Satan a stronghold in our being by not living a habitually sinful lifestyle.

Romans 6:23 – *For the wages of sin is death; but the gift of God is eternal life through Jesus Christ our Lord.*

This memory verse states the stark reality between living for sinful self and living for holy God. It is literally a choice between heaven and hell … forever.

Romans 8:16-18 – *The Spirit itself beareth witness with our spirit, that we are the children of God: 17 – And if children, then heirs; heirs of God, and joint-heirs with Christ; if so be that we suffer with Him, that we may be also glorified together. 18 – For I reckon that the sufferings of this present time are not worthy to be compared with the glory which shall be revealed in us.*

The Holy Spirit agreeing with our spirit is the way we can have steadfast assurance that we <u>do</u> belong to the Lord, and that He holds our ultimate destiny firmly in His trustworthy grip, which no man can pluck us from. Here we are called joint-heirs with God's only begotten Son. A joint-heir shares equally with all other heirs. Jesus is assuring us that, through His sacrifice for us, we hold equal status with Him in the provisions of our heavenly Father. The closing memory verse here tells us the ills and troubles and cares of this mortal life are to be counted as nothing when compared to the rewards in heaven.

Romans 8:28 – *And we know that all things work together for good to them that love God, to them who are the called according to His purpose.*

This most powerful memory verse is a real favorite of my wife. She relies on its wisdom to explain the rough spots we occasionally encounter. It can be a soothing balm to our being, like aloe vera to a sunburned back. Some of the new gee whiz translations render this Scripture with the word "the" between "are ___ called," omitted from the text, changing the context. Called and the called are two different meanings. Anyone can be called – the called are those preordained by God.

Romans 10:9-17 – *That if thou shalt confess with thy mouth the Lord Jesus, and shalt believe in thine heart that God hath raised him from the dead, thou shalt be saved. 10 – For with the heart man believeth unto righteousness; and with the mouth confession is made unto salvation. 11 – For the Scripture sayeth, whosoever believeth on Him shall not be ashamed. 12 – For there is no difference between the Jew and the Greek: for the same Lord over all is rich unto all that call upon Him. 13 – For whosoever shall call upon the name of the Lord shall be saved. 14 – How then shall they call on Him in whom they have not believed? And how shall they believe in Him of whom they have not heard? And how shall they hear without a preacher? 15 – And how shall they preach, except they be sent? As it is written, how beautiful are the feet of them that preach the Gospel of peace, and bring glad tidings of good things! 16 – But they have not all obeyed the Gospel. For Esaias saith, Lord, who hath believed our report? 17 – So then faith cometh by hearing, and hearing by the word of God.*

These memory verses establish that the Lord's offer of salvation is available to everyone, not just certain groups of sects, but everyone! Also we see there are no requirements for intervention by any man or man-made ordinance or rite. No prayers to any saints or

Mother Mary or any such thing. We see plainly where faith in God originates and waxes stronger – with God himself through His word. The question is posed asking how these things can occur without a preacher (I take this to mean a faithful person who teaches … preaches to us.) This, to my understanding, doesn't require a man with a doctorate nor ordination by any sect. The mention of the beauty of the preacher's feet doesn't mean alligator Stacy Adams shoes nor a good pedicure. I feel it is speaking to how welcome a dedicated-to-the-Gospel person is to an occasion where salvation is being discussed. All in all, this is a great bit of Scripture that can be useful when witnessing to the lost.

Romans 12:1-5 – *I beseech you therefore, Brethren, by the mercies of God, that ye present your bodies a living sacrifice, holy, acceptable unto God, which is your reasonable service. 2 – And be not conformed to this world: but be ye transformed by the renewing of your mind, that ye may prove what is that good, and acceptable and perfect will of God. 3 – For I say, through the grace given unto me, to every man that is among you, not to think of himself more highly than he ought to think; but to think soberly, according as God hath dealt to every man the measure of faith. 4 – For as we have many members in one body, and all members have not the sane office: 5 – So we, being many, are one body in Christ, and every one members one of another.*

This portion of Paul's letter to the church in Rome shows Paul's practical application of the Gospel of Jesus Christ. Here he is encouraging the followers of Christ to live in holiness as modeled by Christ while He lived among men. The point is stressed for believers to not be conformed to the evil world we live in. This echos Jesus' earlier admonition for us, although we live in this world, we are not to be of this world (John 17:14-18). Instead of conforming …, adjusting to be like the sinful world, we are to strive to be transformed, changed from, the gutter existence of human depravity. We are admonished to refrain from holding too high opinions of ourselves. This message seems to be wasted on many preachers. He closes this memory Scripture by reminding us we all have different gifts, but are called to render our service in cooperation with all other members.

Romans 13:8 – *Owe no man any thing, but to love one another: for he that loveth another hath fulfilled the law.*

This short memory verse seems to be a sort of short-hand expression of Jesus' telling us His two commandments as recorded at Mark 12:31. The lead off statement about owing no man, could be taken literally as meaning to not borrow from others, where it would agree with Proverbs 22:7

Romans 14:7-13 – *For none of us liveth to himself, and no man dieth to himself. 8 – For whether we live, we live unto the Lord; and whether we die, we die unto the Lord: whether we live therefore, or die, we are the Lord's. 9 – For to this end Christ both died, and rose, and revived, that He might be Lord of both the dead and living. 10 – But why dost thou judge thy brother? Or why dost thou set at naught thy brother? For we shall all stand before the judgment seat of Christ. 11 – For it is written, as I live, saith the Lord, every knee shall bow to me, and every tongue shall confess to God. 12 – So then every one of us shall give account of himself to God. 13 – Let us not therefore judge one another any more: but judge this rather, that no man put a stumbling block or an occasion to fall in his brother's way.*

These memory verses here are Christian human relations 101, in that Jesus is telling us we all live together here on earth. No one is solo, "No man is an island" we say. Christ died for everyone who will beckon to His call. We are not to be judges of our fellowmen, He and He alone is to be the judge of us and others. In the end, everyone – kings-to- paupers, will acknowledge Him as the righteous leader of every living soul. We will each one be held accountable for our actions and omissions. We are called to not be impeding the progress of others, but to love, and help one another in His name.

Romans 15:9 – *And that the Gentiles might glorify God for His mercies; as it is written, for this cause I will confess to thee among the Gentiles, and sing unto thy name.*

Paul's first commission after his salvation was to work bringing the Gospel of Christ to his own people, the Jews. Here in this memory verse, he is citing the will of the Lord that the truth should be shared with the non-Jewish people, the Gentiles. As it turned out, those Gentiles took to the Gospel like the proverbial duck to water, while the majority of the Jews clung to their rights from Abraham and resolutely denied the Deity of Jesus Christ. The practicing Jews of today still refuse to recognize Him as the Messiah.

1 Corinthians 1:18 – *For the preaching of the cross is to them that perish foolishness; but unto us which are saved it is the power of God.*

The unsaved fail to understand the Gospel, and usually have little or no interest in learning the powerful message it contains for them. For this reason it is required that the Holy Spirit works in their hearts, and that we in hoping to help must be gentle with them as we present the need for everyone to repent and accept Jesus' offer for a new, soft heart. The whole thing appears to them to be unnecessary concerns over nothing – foolishness. We, on the other hand, know the importance of the matter, and that we have in the Gospel message the very power of God ..., the power of the One who created the entire universe, ourselves, and the lost soul we are contending for. With the Creator and His Spirit we have the puny devil under our heel. Let us be gentle with the searcher while giving Satan his part, the kingdom of hell.

1 Corinthians 2:14 – *But the natural man receiveth not the things of the Spirit of God: for they are foolishness unto him: neither can he know them, because they are spiritually discerned.*

This memory verse is a strong affirmation and supporting statement to the preceding one. This underlines the importance to God that we understand the crucial need for us to remember the message as it pertains to our efforts to bring the message of salvation to our neighbors – those natural men. We cannot convince them by argument or debate; because, as the Scripture advises us, it is spiritually discerned – understood.

1 Corinthians 6:19-20 – *What? know ye not that your body is the temple of the Holy Ghost which is in you, which ye have of God, and ye are not your own? 20 – For ye are bought with a price: therefore glorify God in your body, and in your spirit, which are God's.*

The secular, headed-for-hell fools, who say there is no God have a battle cry they love to yell to the news cameras and elsewhere - "It's my body, I can do whatever I want with it." It's a waste of our time mostly, to try to tell these self-absorbed ones the truth, but we do it anyway. We are told by the Lord that it is our duty to present the Gospel everywhere – not just among Christian friends. I think almost everyone knows in their heart that they are wrong to start with. Meanwhile, we sometimes need to be reminded, like when it's time to get some beneficial exercise, do some push backs from the table, turn down cheerfully the offer of just one more little slice of pecan pie, etc. If a friend loaned you his new BMW to take on vacation, you wouldn't abuse it. God has loaned us this old tent for three score and ten, we should show our appreciation by taking the best care of it. Let's not forget the Divine extended warranty on our soul and spirit which is good <u>FOREVER</u> which costs us nothing. In case you have neglected that very most important thing, don't delay another minute but go to Him on your knees right now!

1 Corinthians 10:13 – *There hath no temptation taken you but such as is common to man: but God is faithful, who will not suffer you to be tempted above that ye are able; but will with the temptation also make a way to escape, that ye may be able to bear it.*

This memory verse is a wonderful promise from God. A promise to always give His children protection from the temptations of this evil world and its ruler, Satan. Those temptations make the sin offered look so enticing, and so innocent. "nobody will ever know" - "what they don't know won't hurt them" - "it's nobody else's business" - "just this once" - "come on-don't be a party pooper" - "you don't have to make a habit of it" - "look at me, it's not hurting me" - "this may be your last chance" and the excuses go on and on. When Satan offers the forbidden fruit, we know it and our fleshly self desires it, but God has promised to give us an escape route. Tell the devil to go to hell and evoke the name of Jesus, and you <u>will</u> be delivered – praise God.

1 Corinthians 10:31-32 – *Whether therefore ye eat, or drink, or whatsoever ye do, do all to the glory of God. 32-Give none offense, neither to the Jews, nor to the Gentiles, nor to the church of God:*

This memory verse is clear and easily understood. We are to treat others the way we want to be treated. Don't bring a ham to a bar mitzvah, nor pour a Baptist preacher a glass of wine. In all things, such as eating and drinking, do it all to God's glory. Don't do things that are unseemly to others in your company. Practice Jesus' golden rule and give intentional offense to no one. Jesus told us to love one another many times, and this is a reminder to show our love for others by the way we interact with them. Apparently there wasn't a Baptist preacher present among the sizable throng of celebrants at the wedding at Cana as recorded in John, chapter 2.

1 Corinthians 11:24-31 – *And when He had given thanks, He brake it, and said, Take, eat: this is my body, which is broken for you: this do in remembrance of me. 25 – After the same manner also He took the cup, when He had supped, saying, this cup is the new testament in my blood: this do ye, as oft as ye drink it, in remembrance of me. 26 – For as often as ye eat this bread, and drink this cup, ye do shew the Lord's death till He come. 27 – Wherefore whosoever shall eat this bread, and drink this cup of the Lord, unworthily, shall be guilty of the body and blood of the Lord. 28 – But let a man examine himself, and so let him eat of that bread, and drink of that cup. 29 – For he that eateth and drinketh unworthily, eateth and drinketh damnation to himself, not discerning the Lord's body. 30 – For this cause many are weak and sickly among you, and many sleep. 31 – For if we would judge ourselves, we should not be judged.*

These solemn cautionary words here are referring to the observance of the Lord's Supper as it relates to the proper attitude and spiritual condition of those engaging in the holy rite. We are told to not come to this observance while living a sinful, unrepentant lifestyle. The specific warning is that to do so can lead to judgment resulting in sickness and/or death. This admonition here is one of the few cases where New Testament worshipers are given such strong warnings. This is a serious matter – if anyone has questions, they should pray about the matter, and seek counsel with their pastor or other trusted, mature Christian friend. The prayer contained at Psalm 139:23-24 is a worthy outline for us to consider prior to taking the Lord's Supper. Another Scripture which addresses this area is Matthew 5:23-24 where we are instructed to not bring a gift to the altar while a brother has something against us. The closing sentence here is saying if we will judge ourselves responsibly, God will not be required to do it.

1 Corinthians 13:12-13 – *For now we see through a glass, darkly; but then face to face: now I know in part; but then shall I know even as also I am known. 13 – And now abideth faith, hope, charity, these three; but the greatest of these is charity*

This first verse here is something that gives us comfort when we are faced with a question concerning Biblical matters that puzzle us from time to time. The promise contained here is that when we cross Jordan we will have clear understanding, just like those in heaven now have. No more wondering just how the Trinity is arranged … was Jesus fully God when just a baby … and others. The second verse is understood by many scholars to mean love where the KJV says charity. This was true before and after 1604. The Tyndale translation of the New Testament of 1526 translated the Greek "agape" here as love. To me, the word love is broadly based, while charity is one, more narrow form of love. Either way, these are two widely separated truths presented for our edification here.

1 Corinthians 15:17-22 - *And if Christ be not raised, your faith is vain; ye are yet in your sins. 18 – Then they also which are fallen asleep in Christ are perished. 19 – If in this life only we have hope in Christ, we are of all men most miserable. 20 – But now is Christ risen from the dead, and become the firstfruiths of them that slept. 21 – For since by man came death, by man also came resurrection of the dead. 22 – For as in Adam all die, even so in Christ shall all be made alive.*

This memory Scripture tells us that if the story of Christ's resurrection were a fable, then so would be our salvation. It shows, to me, that anyone unbelieving of the resurrection account isn't saved. The tombs and crypts of other religious leaders are to be visited today. The burial place of Jesus Christ stands empty ever since three days after His crucifixion. The sin of Adam brought death to all humanity; the sacrifice of sinless Jesus brings us the opportunity for eternal life with Him in heaven.

1 Corinthians 15:55-58 – *O death, where is thy sting? O grave, where is thy victory? 56 – The sting of death is sin; and the strength of sin is the law. 57 – But thanks be to God, which giveth us the victory through our Lord Jesus Christ. 58 – Therefore, my beloved brethren, be ye steadfast,*

unmovable, always abounding in the work of the Lord, forasmuch as ye know that your work is not in vain in the Lord.

These reassuring words of Scripture are meant as soothing balm to those Christians facing imminent death. These are powerful assurances of His providing ultimate cancellation of the horrors and pain of physical death. He is reminding us that our work for the kingdom will be rewarded in heaven. These words are great solace to those of us who have passed four score years here and are on a short list for departure to cross Jordan.

2 Corinthians 4:18 – *While we look not at the things which are seen, but at the things which are not seen: for the things which are seen are temporal; but the things which are not seen are eternal.*

We all love to waste our lives discussing the things reported in the news media, social networks, and gossip. We spend more time and effort planning a short, week end trip to the beach or woods than we do pondering eternity, which may come before the planned outing. We are reliably told that our lives here on earth are "even as a vapor" (James 4:14). We read the stats on the sports page as if they meant something. Those things, and most of the other "news" are on par with what Dagwood and Herb are doing in the comics. The closing line here reminds us that the things our society ignores have eternal relevance for all of us. We would do our souls a great favor to put the paper in the bird's cage and spend more time in the timeless book of wisdom …, the Bible.

2 Corinthians 5:10 – *For we all must appear before the judgment seat of Christ; that every one may receive the things done in his body, according to that he hath done, whether it be good or bad.*

Everyone should spend their entire life in preparation for this most important event. The things to be judged by Christ – whether they be good or bad, are all done in this lifetime. It appears those matters before salvation are put away "as far as the east is from the west" but our later works – good and bad are to be judged at this time and place. Let us all be storing up in heaven our treasures.

2 Corinthians 5:17 — *Therefore if any man be in Christ, he is a new creature: old things are passed away; behold, all things are become new.*

This little memory verse has a big message. It tells us that when we receive Jesus Christ's free gift of salvation, we do, indeed, become a new and different person. The angels in heaven rejoice every time this occurs here on earth. Sadly, we do retain our old sin nature, but we are to aim for a life of sinlessness and perfection in His likeness. We are to constantly strive to leave those evil acts "passed away."

2 Corinthians 5:21 — *For He hath made Him to be sin for us, who knew no sin; that we might be made the righteousness of God in Him.*

This one sentence memory verse explains the miracle wrought by God through His Son to move our sins onto His account. When we ponder this, it is amazing – a thing only God can do.

2 Corinthians 10:3-5 — *For though we walk in the flesh, we do not war after the flesh: 4 - (For the weapons of our warfare are not carnal, but mighty through God to the pulling down of strongholds:) 5 – Casting down imaginations, and every high thing that exalteth itself against the knowledge of God, and bringing into captivity every thought to the obedience of Christ;*

We often become frustrated when we cannot correct things in our world that are being done in direct opposition to the dictates of God and conscience. We tend to forget the words of Godly wisdom contained here in these memory verses, and attempt to rectify wrongs by direct actions against those who attempt to mock God through their evil, sinful actions. We have been living under an administration for several years which fits the descriptions given in verse 5 here. They ignore the realities of the world condition while living in the imaginations of their ideologies and fancied fairyland. They surely exalt themselves while denying the things of God, even to removing all reference to Him in public places under their evil control. We cannot prevail against their devil-designed onslaught in their evil courts, but in God's halls of justice.

2 Corinthians 11:25 – *Thrice was I beaten with rods, once was I stoned, thrice I suffered shipwreck, a night and a day I have been in the deep;*

Here Paul is telling his readers of some of the hardships he has endured since his experience with Jesus on the road to Damascus that led to Paul's conversion. He was neither bragging nor complaining here; just stating the facts. He didn't even mention the many difficulties he experienced with the people he dealt with nor the persistent thorn in the flesh he asked God three times to relieve him from. His statement here flies in the face of modernistic, feel good, church teaching that good Christians should never experience any kinds of hardships or suffering. Our rewards are stored up in heaven, where we should be sending our treasures also.

2 Corinthians 12:7-10 – *And lest I should be exalted above measure through the abundance of the revelations, there was given to me a thorn in the flesh, the messenger of Satan to buffet me, lest I should be exalted above measure. 8 – For this thing I besought the Lord thrice, that it might depart from me. 9 – And He said unto me, my grace is sufficient for thee: for my strength is made perfect in weakness. Most gladly therefore will I rather glory in my infirmities, that the power of Christ may rest upon me. 10 – Therefore I take pleasure in infirmities, in reproaches, in necessities, in persecutions, in distresses for Christ's sake: for when I am weak, then am I strong.*

These four memory verses buttress and amplify the previous ones in 11:25. We see here that Paul accepted God's decision regarding that thorn in the flesh as his permanent bug-a-boo to tolerate. Bible expositors have speculated widely on just what that particular condition was, from ingrown toe nails to poor eyesight. It really doesn't matter, but I would guess kidney stones, hemorrhoids, or gout. Anyway, the message here is that when we are weak in self-worth, we are strong in the Lord. Weak in self-image is to be humble, like Jesus was in His composure when dealing with His flock. When we are glorying in self-adoration and pride is when we are at greatest peril and apt to stumble. These things agree with one another throughout the entire Bible.

Galatians 2:20 – *I am crucified with Christ: nevertheless I live; yet not I, but Christ liveth in me: and the life which I now live in the flesh I live by the faith of the Son of God, who loved me, and gave Himself for me.*

This is, I think, one of our most beautiful memory verses; in fact one of the sweetest in the Bible. It stipulates the new man is not living for himself, but living for his Savior. It then shows the new life in Him is a new and different existence. The closing words remind us of His supreme gift to all who receive Him as Savior and co-heir in His kingdom in heaven.

Galatians 5:16-17 – *This I say then, Walk in the spirit, and ye shall not fulfil the lust of the flesh. 17 – For the flesh lusteth against the spirit, and the spirit against the flesh: and these are contrary the one to the other: so that ye cannot do the things that ye would.*

Here we see Paul lamenting the fact we all have seen displayed in our own and others' lives. Although God has given us new hearts not made of stone, we have retained our old Adamic lusts, which we must continually resist. If anyone feels they have achieved perfection and sinless life, they should consider if perhaps they may have forgotten their wading of the Jordan, and are now living in heaven. As long as we see sin and evil surrounding us, we are still here in this old corrupt world and no one, including ourselves, are perfect. We must keep striving to be able to do only those things we would, while remembering we never attain that lofty goal here and now.

Galatians 5:22-23 – *But the fruit of the spirit is love, joy, peace, longsuffering, gentleness, goodness, faith, 23 – Meekness, temperance: against such there is no law.*

This memory verse is God's check list; His litmus test, His gold standard, His benchmark to determine whether people we meet are truly sheep of His pasture, or wolves of the world, in sheepskins. We classify people based on outward appearances while He looks on their hearts. (1 Samuel 16:7). Here, in this passage we find a code, if you will, to use enabling us to see others with more of God's insight to help us tell the sheep from the goats. Compare this specific list of human assets with the wisdom taught in Psalm 1, and see the parallel criteria.

Galatians 6:7-10 – *Be not deceived; God is not mocked: for whatsoever a man soweth, that shall he also reap. 8 – For he that soweth to his flesh shall of the flesh reap corruption; but he that soweth to the spirit shall of the spirit reap life everlasting. 9 – And let us not be weary in well doing; for in due season we shall reap, if we faint not. 10 – As we have therefore opportunity, let us do good unto all men, especially unto them who are of the household of faith.*

This great teaching Scripture has several connected kernels of Godly wisdom for our edification. The first is the admonition that God will not tolerate saint nor sinner to make attempts to make fun of Him. When we hear some unbeliever jesting concerning the things of God and/or His kingdom, we should remove ourselves quickly; there could easily be a bolt of lightning as an exclamation point to the revelry. We also see that those who sow corruption will be rewarded by corruption. If we sow bluebonnets we can expect bluebonnets, If we sow barley we will get barley. Recently one of our sons and his wife were traveling by car from Oklahoma into Texas when they saw prolific amounts of bluebonnets beside the highway soon after entering Texas. The question was, why such a difference upon crossing the state line? The answer is the efforts of the Texas Highway Department's policy of sowing bluebonnet seeds beside the Texas roadways every year. The closing thought is to do good to everyone, especially those who are fellow Christians.

Ephesians 2:8-10 – *For by grace are ye saved through faith; and that not of yourselves: it is the gift of God: 9 – Not of works, lest any man should boast. 10 – For we are His workmanship, created in Christ Jesus unto good works, which God hath before ordained that we should walk in them.*

This could rightfully be called the invisible text of the Bible, because so many different denominations have so many, many different "works" they insist must be accomplished in order to receive/retain salvation. Some stipulate church mandated study courses; some insist baptism or other rites must be done. Others cite the abstinence from some particular practices such as consuming alcohol, dancing. growing facial hair on men, wearing no head covering by women, eating pork or other proscribed items, working on Sunday, etc. Verse 9 speaks of "lest any man should boast," which could be spoken and written as, "lest millions of men should boast." Some members of a protestant church group my mother's family was associated with have such a multitude of things that must be observed to "keep their salvation" as to be saddening. If they are correct in their doctrine, there cannot be enough of them in heaven to comprise a basketball team since their sect originated just a few generations ago! Man, in his selfish pride, just thinks he must reserve a little glory, even if it blasphemes God.

Ephesians 4:31-32 – *Let all bitterness, and wrath, and anger, and clamor, and evil speaking, be put away from you, with all malice: 32 – And be ye kind one to another, tenderhearted, forgiving one another, even as God for Christ's sake hath forgiven you.*

If everyone everywhere were to put these words into practice, the world's troubles would vanish like waste when we pull the chain or flip the lever in the bathroom. Even if only those who read it, or just married couples practiced it, peace would come to most of the planet. This is a memory verse my dear wife has quoted to her husband a few times when she wasn't just practicing, and with just cause and favorable results. These attributes listed here should be thought of as minimum standards of behavior by born again Christians.

Ephesians 5:18 – *And be not drunk with wine, wherein is excess; but be filled with the spirit;*

This short memory verse is full of divine wisdom which should be carefully considered as to just what is being taught. It says for us to not be DRUNK with wine: it doesn't tell us to not be drinking wine. There IS a difference and many preachers of some denominations refuse to recognize the important difference. When Jesus made over a hundred gallons of "good wine" as recorded in John, chapter two, He undoubtedly made it for the people to drink, but not to become drunk, from over indulgence. Jesus is the same yesterday, today and forever. What He expected of His mother and the rest of the people yesterday, He expects of us today. The verse closes by reminding us to stay filled with the Spirit.

Ephesians 5:25-33 – *Husbands, love your wives, even as Christ also loved the church, and gave himself for it; 26 – That He might sanctify and cleanse it with the washing of water by the word, 27 – That He might present it to himself a glorious church, not having spot, or wrinkle, or any such thing; but that it should be holy and without blemish. 28 – So ought men to love their wives as their own bodies. He that loveth his wife loveth himself. 29 – For no man ever yet hateth his own flesh; but nourisheth and cherisheth it, even as the Lord the church: 30 – For we are members of His body, of His flesh, and of His bones. 31 – For this cause shall a man leave his father and mother, and shall be joined unto his wife, and they two shall be one flesh. 32 – This is a great mystery: But I speak concerning Christ and the church. 33 – Nevertheless let every one of you in particular so love his wife even as himself; and the wife see that she reverence her husband.*

This rather long memory study covers the absolute protection of every marriage against the divorce which God hates. Notice we aren't instructed to love ourselves, God knows we already do that. We are instructed to love our wives equally with our love of self. If a husband does that, then his dear wife will have no trouble reverencing him quite naturally. Comparing a man's love for his wife to Christ's love for His church puts the man's love for his wife in the very strongest terms – Christ died on the cross for His church and every member thereof. Let me reiterate; if every husband faithfully followed these instructions, the divorce lawyers would be forced to find honorable work. Paul just touches on the fact that a young man will very naturally leave the home of his youth when he finds a wife.

Ephesians 6:4 – *And, ye fathers, provoke not your children to wrath: but bring them up in the nurture and admonition of the lord.*

We are told elsewhere that parents who love their children will use the rod to chasten them as needed. Here we are told in no uncertain terms, to not overdo it. No child nor adult, for that matter, wants to be chastised nor punished. When that adverseness becomes righteous wrath the bounds of reason have been surpassed. The available cure for such is a heartfelt apology to the child …,and to the Lord.

Ephesians 6:10-17 – *Finally, my brethren, be strong in the Lord, and in the power of His might. 11 – put on the whole armor of God, that ye may be able to stand against the wiles of the devil. 12 – For we wrestle not against flesh and blood, but against principalities, against powers, against the rulers of the darkness of this world, against spiritual wickedness in high places. 13 – Wherefore take unto you the whole armor of God, that ye may be able to withstand in the evil day, and having done all, to stand. 14 – Stand therefore, having your loins girt about with truth, and having on the breastplate of righteousness; 15 – And your feet shod with the preparation of the Gospel of peace; 16 – Above all, taking the shield of faith, wherewith ye shall be able to quench all the fiery darts of the wicked. 17 – And take the helmet of salvation, and the sword of the spirit, which is the word of God.*

These strongly worded memory verses are a favorite bit of Scripture to Shirley, she sees the answers to most of the evil world's problems right here in God's word. I can easily agree with her, since Paul's insightful description here makes such a clear comparison between a warrior's equipment and the things helpful to us in our Christian walk. The heartless Roman rule of that day and our present situation share many, many similarities. It's true all over the wicked world, and as much so here in our nation as anywhere. The rot starts at the top. We suffer under a godless regime of wanton leadership who mislead our people in godless misadventures leading to our doom. We are here reminded the problems we face aren't made up of flesh and blood – humanity – but evil forces led by Satan. The evil men involved are mere spineless dupes, doing the will of the devil for the mess of pottage of satisfying their lusts for power.

Philippians 1:21 – *For me to live is Christ, and to die is gain.*

This short memory verse is poignant with wisdom. It tells us that living for Christ is everything, surpassing in importance everything else, since such living is showing our love for God, which is the first and great commandment of Christ. It also reminds us that our earthly death leads directly to a much better life in heaven. These are two great truths – truths that do indeed set us free.

Philippians 2:5-9 – *Let this mind be in you, which was also in Christ Jesus: 6 – Who, being in the form of God, thought it not robbery to be equal with God: 7 – But made himself of no reputation, and took upon him the form of a servant, and was made in the likeness of men: 8 – And being found in fashion as a man, he humbled himself, and became obedient unto death, even the death on the cross. 9 – Wherefore God also hath highly exalted him, and given him a name which is above every name:*

This powerful memory Scripture fully explains the relative positions of God the Father and God the Son. They are co-equal and in complete harmony, agreeing in everything. The writer of the Koran of Islam must have never read this. (having just typed the preceding, I was reminded that Mohammed was illiterate, hence unable to read.) These verses here establish exactly the relationship between the Father and the Son.

Philippians 2:13 – *For it is God which worketh in you both to will and to do of His good pleasure.*

This very concise memory verse reminds us that <u>any</u> good thing we might ever do, comes from God, not us. Of course, it is all too human for us to pridefully take credit for anything we are even near to which is a good deed. Whenever we see someone bragging on themselves we should remember their tongue is being controlled by the devil.

Philippians 3;13-14 – *Brethren, I count not myself to have apprehended: but this one thing I do, forgetting those things which are behind, and reaching forth unto those things which are before, 14 – I press toward the mark for the prize of the high calling of God in Christ Jesus.*

Paul speaks here as like one who is referring to a foot race. He encourages us to not dwell on the past, and to look forward to what we may be able to accomplish that is worthy of our efforts in kingdom matters.

Philippians 3;20-21 – *For our conversation is in heaven; from whence also we look for the Savior, the Lord Jesus Christ: 21 – who shall change our vile body, that it may be fashioned like unto His glorious body, according to the working whereby He is able even to subdue all things unto himself.*

This promise here is our expectation of a heavenly exchange of this old tent we have been trying to keep patched up with the doctors' help, these many years, for a new-improved, perfected model. Heaven would be a great blessing even if we still had to use pain control medicine, blood thinners, and pacemakers; but none of such things will be needed there. Without needing hearing aids, glasses, and dentures we will feel as if we have been freed from prison!

Philippians 4:4-8 – Rejoice in the Lord alway: and again I say, Rejoice. 5 – Let your moderation be known unto all men. The Lord is at hand. 6 – Be careful for nothing; but in everything by prayer and supplication with thanksgiving let your requests be made known unto God. 7 – And the peace of God, which passeth all understanding, shall keep your hearts and minds through Christ Jesus. 8 – Finally, brethren, whatsoever things are true, whatsoever things are honest, whatsoever things are just, whatsoever things are pure, whatsoever things are lovely, whatsoever things are of good report; if there be any virtue, and if there be any praise, think on these things.

We can learn much truth about how we should comport ourselves to have a better life here in this evil world. My dear mother used to say we should practice "moderation in all things," and as I grew older I heard these exact four words over and over. I was surprised when I looked for the phrase in Strong's Exhaustive Concordance. This passage here is the only use of the word "moderation" in the KJV although the concept is inferred many times as a good practice. The list of "whatsoevers" are a good checklist for happy living. As we memorize this list, let's put it into daily practice.

Philippians 4:11-13 – Not that I speak in respect of want: for I have learned, in whatsoever state I am, therewith to be content. 12 – I know both how to be abased, and I know how to abound: every where and in all things I am instructed both to be full and to be hungry, both to abound and to suffer need. 13 – I can do all things through Christ which strenghteneth me.

The Apostle Paul had already lived a much varied life by the time he wrote this epistle to the church flock at Philippi. In fact, he was in prison in Rome when he wrote this letter to his favorite people. Paul was raised, a Roman citizen, in a wealthy Jewish family, studied under the premier teacher of the day, and was a member of the ruling party, As we have read earlier, he also suffered many injustices and deprivations. Here he closes this informative Scripture and says he can do anything through the power of Christ.

Philippians 4:19 – *But my God shall supply all your need according to His riches in glory by Christ Jesus.*

This is a very small memory verse with a very big message. This is a promise from God through the pen of Paul, promising to fulfill all our needs for eternity. To my way of thinking, this is the broadest, highest, greatest promise ever!

Colossians 1:9-13 – *For this cause we also, since the day we heard it, do not cease to pray for you, and to desire that ye might be filled with the knowledge of His will in all wisdom and spiritual understanding; 10 – That ye might walk worthy of the Lord unto all pleasing, being fruitful in every good work, and increasing in the knowledge of God; 11 – Strenghtened with all might, according to His glorious power, unto all patience and long suffering with joyfulness; 12 – Giving thanks unto the Father, which hath made us meet to be partakers of the inheritance of the saints in light: 13 – Who hath delivered us from the power of darkness, and hath translated us into the kingdom of His dear Son:*

This passage of Scripture is part of the salutation of Paul's letter to the church at Colosse, where he was instructing them concerning keeping other teachings from polluting the Gospel of Christ. Paul shows his care for the people and their walk in the light of truth. We can take his words here as a model for our dealings with one another. Bible study classes and prayer meetings, where the progress of other Christians are stressed are two ways we can pursue the spreading of His word.

Colossians 2:11-12 – *In whom also ye are circumcised with the circumcision made without hands, in putting off the body of the sins of the flesh by the circumcision of Christ: 12 – Buried with Him in baptism, wherein also ye are risen with Him through the faith of the operation of God, who hath raised Him from the dead.*

Paul is telling us here that the Gospel of Christ is all we have need of in receiving salvation. Thus he is saying Jesus Christ is all that we have need of, and that our faith should be in Him rather than the rituals of the law. This was a major snag for those raised in Jewish tradition at the time. I feel the message here for us today, is to follow God's will in our lives and not the traditions of men.

Colossians 3:12-13 – *Put on therefore, as the elect of God, holy and beloved, bowels of mercies, kindness, humbleness of mind, meekness, longsuffering; 13 – Forebearing one another, and forgiving one another, if any man have a quarrel against any: even as Christ forgave you, so also do ye.*

This Scripture teaches the same message as Jesus taught in His sermon on the mount, to have His followers show love and compassion towards one another, as well as others. The world's attitude is exactly opposite to these words here. The world's fastest expanding religion teaches hatred and vengeance to everyone outside of their group. We are called to forgive others in humbleness and love.

Colossians 3:16 - *Let the word of Christ dwell in you richly in all wisdom; teaching and admonishing one another in psalms and hymns and spiritual songs, singing with grace in your hearts to the Lord.*

This memory verse seems easily understood and complied with. We are being told to stay in the Word with vigor and gaining Godly wisdom therefrom. We are also told to teach and admonish fellow believers with singing. I suppose this gem of Scripture was accidentally omitted from the texts of those who teach we are to have no music in the church house. Anyway, I'm happy we have the authority of the Lord for these practices; even though I personally cannot sing with much grace. I still thank the Lord for those around me who can, and do sing gracefully …, and on key.

Collossians 3:23-25 – *And whatsoever ye do, do it heartily, as to the Lord, and not unto men; 24 – Knowing that of the Lord ye shall receive the reward of the inheritance: for ye serve the Lord Christ. 25 – But he that doeth wrong shall receive for the wrong which he hath done: and there is no respect of persons.*

These three memory verses cover a lot of ground. First, we see we are not to just do our job to please the boss, but to do things in a manner to please the Lord. Some earthly overseers are hard to please, but God knows when we are doing our best, and He is thus pleased with our work. The inheritance spoken of here is our rewards in heaven where we are co-heirs with Christ. The reference to wrong deeds is a reminder that we reap what we sow. That short mention of respect for persons means, to me, that in God's judgment hall we are all equal – prince or pauper. We need not concern ourselves with the world's high and mighty rulers who mistreat men and mock God here and now ...,they won't be there to be considered anyway.

1 Thessalonians 4:16-18 – *For the Lord himself shall descend from heaven with a shout, with the voice of the archangel, and with the trump of God: and the dead in Christ shall rise first: 17 – Then we which are alive and remain shall be caught up together with them in the clouds to meet the Lord in the air: and so shall we ever be with the Lord. 18 – Wherefore comfort one another with these words.*

This is what Shirley calls the "rapture" verses, because it contains the promises given to us regarding what many Christians refer to as the rapture of the saints, dead and alive, at the time of Christ's return. The "trump" of God mentioned has nothing to do with a bridge game nor an outspoken casino operator. It refers to the trumpet of God, probably a sound of a great musical horn heard worldwide to announce this unique event of Biblical prophesy. Those believers who are alive during this momentous occasion will see the graves of the dead emptied as those resurrected saints precede them in joining Jesus Christ for eternity. The closing words here encourage Shirley and others to discuss this heavenly phenomenon, which she does frequently and with enthusiasm.

1 Thessalonians 5:17-23 – *Pray without ceasing. 18 – In everything give thanks: for this is the will of God in Christ Jesus concerning you. 19 – Quench not the Spirit. 20 – Despise not prophesyings. 21 – Prove all things; hold fast that which is good. 22 – Abstain from all appearance of evil. 23 – And the very God of peace sanctify you wholly; and I pray God your whole spirit and soul and body be preserved blameless unto the coming of our Lord Jesus Christ.*

What a great collection of good instructions in such a limited space! The first kernel of wisdom and truth reminds us to not just pray before meals, at bedtime, and when we get ourselves in a jam. Our Christian lives should be a constant, prayerful attitude. When we do things without prayer, we are in danger of doing wrong. We should never fail to be thankful to God for all good things, and thankful to others when they offer help. We should never do or think anything that causes the Holy Spirit any discomfort in any way. We should have an interest in and an appreciation for the words of the prophets – old and modern – male and female. Check things out, using God's word as your bench mark; keeping the good kernels, and discarding the worldly chaff. If something looks bad or sinful drop it like a hot potato, offending no one. Observance of these tenets makes the Lord happy, and us as well.

2 Thessalonians 3:10 – *For even when we were with you, this we commanded you, that if any would not work, neither should he eat.*

This teaching here is simple, direct, and unambiguous. Why do liberals, who claim to be Christians forever insist it is uncaring? This is a natural law of economics instituted by God that is as sure as His law of physics that we call gravity. Just as water obeys gravity and runs downhill, so should we obey the Garden of Eden edict of God, that we must earn our food by the sweat of our brows. The government policies that encourage fit citizens to skip work and live on the public dole are in direct opposition to God's best plan for us.

1 Timothy 3:5 – (For if a man know not how to rule his own house, how shall he take care of the church of God?)

Have you ever known a preacher, who let his wife run the church and the police chastise his kids? Such a man will, by God's word here, be a poor pastor. God gave a unique job assignment to women – mothers, and it was not as head of the house nor pastor of His church. Henpecked men are a comedian's foil, but sad failures as preachers tending to God's church.

1 Timothy 3:16 – *And without controversy great is the mystery of godliness: God was manifest in the flesh, justified in the spirit, seen of*

angles, preached unto the Gentiles, believed on in the world, received up into glory.

This Scripture is contained in Paul's letter to young Timothy, where the aging apostle had been recounting the criteria for church officers. Here he is recalling the brief life of Jesus on earth, and enumerating the several events of His ministry. Timothy was preparing to travel and speak among crowds, where intimate knowledge of Christ's teachings was relatively unknown. It is good for us that these facts are here in the Bible to buttress our own knowledge of Jesus' ministry.

1 Timothy 6:10 – *For the love of money is the root of all evil: which while some coveted after, they have erred from the faith, and pierced themselves through with many sorrows.*

Bible revisers seem to dislike this gem of truth in the KJV for some reason. Some new age versions change it to say "all kinds of evil" or "some evils" while others attempt to have the word "love" modified with conditional words such as "too" or "unnatural" etc. This statement of truth here needs no editing, it needs only to be believed and the practice avoided. The love of money seems to contain in itself shards of pride, envy, covetousness and greed. It is as universally practiced in human events as breathing. To call it a root is very accurate. It supports, anchors and feeds a multitude of other sins in mankind.

2 *Timothy 1:7 – For God hath not given us the spirit of fear; but of power, and of love, and of a sound mind.*

Did we get all three of the good things God supplies us with? That power is His power, through Christ, not power in and of ourselves. Jesus told us at John 15:5b that without Him, we can do nothing. The love mentioned here is the same love we are to extend to everyone, even our enemies. The sound mind we have is from God, also, and is not to be misused or abused. The one thing spoken of here is fear, that doesn't come from God, so where does it come from? Fear comes from the devil and is sin. The most powerful instinct in us and lower animals is self-preservation, and it is God-sent. The fear discussed here is the fear we suffer from because we lack sufficient faith in God's provision for us. If we harbor the devil's fear, we only have to ask God for proper faith, and it will vanish.

2 Timothy 1:12 – *For the which cause I also suffer these things: nevertheless I am not ashamed: for I know whom I have believed, and am persuaded that He is able to keep that which I have committed unto Him against that day.*

These things Paul refers to here are his credentials as a preacher, an apostle, and a teacher under Christ. He further shows complete confidence in Jesus' ability to insure his salvation, and protect his soul and spirit for eternity. These are comforting assurances to all believers in our present troubled and evil times.

2 Timothy 2:15 – *Study to shew thyself approved unto God, a workman that needeth not to be ashamed, rightly dividing the word of truth.*

We should live every day in such manner as to be approved by our benevolent Creator. We should glory in whatever work He has provided for each day. Our neo-modern, politically correct society spurns work as being beneath their dignity, and oh-so 1950ish. They go to the gym and pedal bolted-to-the-floor bikes, and feverishly row out-of-water boats to develop their abs and pecs of which they are so peacock-proud. You will never see them working to rid the weeds in their gardens nor their narcissistic lives. In doing so, they, in effect, attempt to mock God. The important closing words pertain to studying God's word – the Bible, under the tutelage of His Spirit.

2 Timothy 3:16-17 – *All Scripture is given by inspiration of God, and is profitable for doctrine, for reproof, for correction, for instruction in righteousness: 17 – That the man of God may be perfect, thoroughly furnished unto all good works.*

If one believes the Bible, this Scripture for memory is the validation stamp of God as it attests to its entire truth. If someone doubts, refer them to this holy "proof of purchase" passage.

Titus 3:5 – *Not by works of righteousness which we have done, but according to His mercy He saved us, by the washing of regeneration, and renewing of the Holy Ghost:*

This is another of the many times we are reminded that our salvation – our regeneration is wholly, totally a work of our Savior, and that we had NO PART in it in ANY WAY. Of course, God knows how prideful we are so these red flags are sprinkled throughout the Bible as reminders.

Philemon 1:17 – *If thou count me therefore a partner, receive him as myself.*

In this short memory verse Paul, a prisoner himself at the time, is imploring his friend, Philemon, to take back his runaway slave, Onesimus, without penalty. This is a good picture of how Christ redeems lost sinners, and enshrines us in an improved set of circumstances. Paul is showing true Christian love and concern here for another believer while Paul himself is incarcerated awaiting his appearance before Caesar, and a possible death sentence. This small book of the Bible is a unique chapter in the apostle's interesting life. You might read, or reread it today.

Hebrews 4:12-25 – *For the Word of God is quick, and powerful, and sharper than any two edged sword, piercing even to the dividing asunder of soul and spirit, and of the joints and marrow, and is a discerner of the thoughts and intents of the heart. 13 – Neither is there any creature that is not manifest in His sight: but all things are naked and opened unto the eyes of Him with whom we have to do. 14 – Seeing then that we have a great high priest, that is passed into the heavens, Jesus the son of God, let us hold fast our profession. 15 – For we have not an high priest which cannot be touched with the feelings of our infirmities; but was in all points tempted like as we are, yet without sin, 16 – Let us therefore come boldly unto the throne of grace, that we may obtain mercy, and find grace to help in time of need.*

This somewhat long memory quotation has, in its first verse one of the longest sentences in the Bible, at forty-four words. It establishes for believers the unique properties of God's word, which it speaks of as a weapon of warfare. It tells us God is all-seeing and all-knowing and that the secrets of man are all laid bare and open to His discerning eyes. It assures us that our Savior – our high priest, although ascended into heaven, is ever with us. It touches on the fact of truth that Jesus understands our temptations, having experienced them himself, and that He resisted them all, to live a sinless life here on planet earth, The closing coda here assures us that we have the right to approach Jesus with our prayers and supplications, as co-heirs with Him.

Hebrews 10:24-25 — *And let us consider one another to provoke unto love and to good works: 25 — Not forsaking the assembling of ourselves together, as the manner of some is; but exhorting one another: and so much the more, as we see the day approaching.*

This memory Scripture is the call to gather at the church house and sing and hear some good preaching. It tells us the loner, who wants to always remove himself from others has a problem that flies in the face of the instructions here. I for some unknown reason recall exactly where it was, that I first memorized this particular Scripture. Shirley and I were on our way from San Antonio to El Remolino, Mexico located some forty miles west of Piedras Negras, Mexico which is cross river from Eagle Pass, Texas. It was approaching Christmas as we stopped at the HEB supermarket in Eagle Pass. While she shopped for supplies including several frozen turkeys, I sat in the car in the parking lot committing these verses to memory. In the years following, when quoting this passage, I am reminded of that scene of years past.

Hebrews 11:1 — *Now faith is the substance of things hoped for, the evidence of things not seen.*

This is the very best description and explanation of precisely what faith is. We need not just understand what faith is; we need to also recognize that faith comes to us from our Maker through reading of His word, through prayer, and through confirming life experiences.

Hebrews 11:6 — *But without faith it is impossible to please Him: for he that cometh to God must believe that He is, and that he is a rewarder of them that diligently seek Him.*

Our preceding memory verse told us what faith is. This one tells us why it is important. We can fool other people about our faith and many other things. However, we cannot fool God in this or any other matter. We can even fool ourselves concerning things we don't want to admit, but God looks on the heart while we can only see outward appearances.

Hebrews 12:5-6 – *And ye have forgotten the exhortation which speaketh unto you as unto children, My son, despise not thou the chastening of the Lord, nor faint when thou art rebuked of Him: 6 – For whom the Lord loveth He chasteneth, and scourgeth every son whom He receiveth.*

We see plainly here that the Lord does jerk our chain whenever we err in our ways. We should recognize His actions for what they are, and repent humbly with resolve to not see what more He might do if we stubbornly or forgetfully repeat the infraction. Elsewhere in God's word, we are told that earthly parents should emulate God's practice with their children.

Hebrews 13:8 – *Jesus Christ the same yesterday, and to day, and for ever.*

Those who have suffered through many of my discourses will recognize this as a favorite memory verse of mine. As men change their laws and ignore them it is a great assurance to me and others that our Lord and Savior is steadfast and unchanging. The Koran of Islam has frequent changes made with the rule being the new position nullifies the older commandment. The church of Rome has Bulls issued by papal authority, which they contend are of equal authority with Holy Scripture. The Mormon church adopts new and varied church laws quite often. Every new age version of the Bible has numerous changes introduced which serve to confuse some Sunday services on par with the constructors of the tower of Babel. Aren't we glad we serve a Savior, who got it all right in the beginning?!

Hebrews 13:15-16 – *By Him therefore let us offer the sacrifice of praise to God continually, that is, the fruit of our lips giving thanks to his name. 16 – But to do good and to communicate forget not: for with such sacrifices God is well pleased.*

We no longer must bring sacrifices of blood to the altar. Jesus made that sacrifice of His precious blood on Calvary's cross for all of us, even as many as will receive Him. The proper and only sacrifice for us today is our words and actions of obedient service.

James 1:22 – *But be ye doers of the word, and not hearers only, deceiving your own selves.*

This is an important Scripture which merits our attention. It is commanding us to be "walkers of the walk" and not merely "talkers of the talk" so to speak. Look at the closing words - that deceiving ourselves is what we were addressing earlier about people being such deceivers they sometimes believe their own propaganda.

James 4:6-8 - *But He giveth more grace. Wherefore He saith, God resisteth the proud, but giveth grace unto the humble. 7 – Submit yourselves therefore to God. Resist the devil, and he will flee from you. 8 – Draw nigh to God, and He will draw nigh to you. Cleanse your hands, ye sinners; and purify your hearts, ye double minded.*

These two memory verses speak of our need to be submissive to God and His will for our benefit, and the truth that if we spurn the devil's temptations in Jesus' name, he will flee. Stressed, is the truth that when we seek closer communion with God, He reciprocates in becoming closer and even more real to us. The closing is telling us to approach God with no hidden agenda, but with guiltless motives and single mindedness.

James 4:13-17 – *Go to now, ye that say, To day or tomorrow we will go into such a city, and continue there a year, and buy and sell, and get gain: 14 – Whereas ye know not what shall be on the morrow. For what is your life? It is even a vapour, that appeareth for a little time, and then vanisheth away. 15 – For that ye ought to say, if the Lord will, we shall live, and do this, or that. 16 – But now ye rejoice in your boastings: all such boasting is evil. 17 – Therefore to him that knoweth to do good, and doeth it not, to him it is sin.*

This is something many think unimportant. If corrected they say a dismissive, "oh yeah" as if everyone should understand they meant it that way. God's last words in this memory Scripture says it is SIN. We once heard a local pastor proudly remark, "We will baptize her

Thursday night." No one corrected him since he reacts badly to even well-meant correction. There should be no hesitation on the part of a Christian in saying "we plan, our hope is, or if the Lord wills," after all without Him we can do nothing.

James 5:16 – *Confess your faults one to another, and pray one for another, that ye may be healed. The effectual fervent prayer of a righteous man availeth much.*

"Confession is good for the soul," is a popular expression used in our secular society, and validated here in Scripture. In the exact context here it pertains to practice among believers. We are instructed also to pray for one another for healing. This can be physical, spiritual and other kinds of healing. The closing thought assures us that the prayers of our saints are effective through the benevolence of our Savior.

1 Peter 3:15 – *But sanctify the Lord God in your hearts: and be ready always to give an answer to every man that asketh you a reason of the hope that is in you with meekness and fear.*

We are here instructed to welcome inquiries concerning our Christian walk from others. This is an important part of taking the Gospel to the unsaved everywhere.

1 Peter 5:6-8 – *Humble yourselves therefore under the mighty hand of God, that He may exalt you in due time: 7 – Casting all your care upon Him; for He careth for you. 8 – Be sober, be vigilant; because your adversary the devil, as a roaring lion, walketh about, seeking whom he may devour:*

This memory Scripture clearly defines the differences between God and Satan. God cares for and loves His children, who are called to be humble and trusting of Him. Conversely, our adversary – Satan busies himself in trying to entice us to fill his domain – hell.

2 Peter 1:21 – *For the prophesy came not in old time by the will of man: but holy men of God spake as they were moved by the Holy Ghost.*

This memory verse tells us where our Bible came from and by whose authority. Holy God through the Holy Spirit gave the exact words He desired to appear in His Holy Writ, for the instruction of His people for hundreds of generations. When we today read or quote words and phrases from the Bible, we are repeating the words and thoughts of very God!

2 Peter 2:1 – *But there were false prophets also among the people, even as there shall be false teachers among you, who privily shall bring in damnable heresies, even denying the Lord that bought them, and bring upon themselves swift destruction.*

It seems as if liars have been prevalent among mankind, since the serpent lied to Eve in the Garden of Eden. That was Satan in the serpent then, and it is he, who causes us to lie to one another and ourselves even today. We have people in leadership positions today spouting damnable heresies to the people. Rick Warren has made millions in recent years writing books for the gullible. He leads an idiotic movement to combine the Gospel of life of Jesus Christ with the death cult of Islam. We have some of our largest churches being led by pastors who preach investment planning religion, telling their flocks and television viewers to send them money, and it will be returned to them by God in multiples with good health and popularity included as a bonus. They are all promised swift destruction.

2 Peter 3:9 – *The Lord is not slack considering His promise, as some men count slackness; but is long suffering to us-ward, not willing that any should perish, but that all should come to repentance.*

Here is the answer to the pundit's question about whether or not God is concerned about everyone's final destination. God, we see, never runs late nor forgets a commitment. Ever hear some unthinking person say, "Well, we just got ahead of God in our enthusiasm," implying God was a laggard? They probably don't mean it to reflect badly on God, but they were a little ahead, so someone had to be running late. God wants everyone to come to Him, and He is patient beyond human ability.

1 John 1:7-9 – *But if we walk in the light, as He is in the light, we have fellowship one with another, and the blood of Jesus Christ His*

Son cleanseth us from all sin. 8 – If we say that we have no sin, we deceive ourselves, and the truth is not in us. 9 – If we confess our sins, He is faithful and just to forgive us our sins, and to cleanse us from all unrighteousness.

Even if one could eschew all the sins of the flesh he would be so eaten up with pride as to not be able to contain himself – and the sin of pride is a black trait of sinful man which spawns seas of other sins. One area pastor a few years ago became so impressed with himself and another, older man in the church that he was heard to tell the congregation that the duo were living sinless lives. This was about the same time he could be seen with a chaw of terbacky in his mouth as he dutifully went about mowing the grass on the church building's lawn. In more polite language verse eight says such people are lying to others.

1 John 2:15-16 – *Love not the world, neither the things that are in the world. If any man love the world, the love of the Father is not in him. 16 – For all that is in the world, the lust of the flesh, the lust of the eyes, and the pride of life, is not of the Father, but is of the world.*

This memory Scripture is one I need to review in my mind every day – sometimes more than once in a given day. If we cannot refrain from overly admiring the things of man and the world; then we should always remember, where all good things come from. When we are so filled with self-awe as we pilot an airplane over tall mountains, we need to remember who made it all possible. Instead of taking pride in our accomplishments, we should give credit where credit is due. Without Him there would be no mountains, airplanes nor egoistical pilots. Whenever we learn a new procedure or work application, we need to thank Him in earnest prayer instead of loudly proclaiming "Look at what I figured out." Remember, if something is of the world, it is not of God – and there's only one other source – Satan.

1 John 4:4 – *Ye are of God, little children, and have overcome them: because greater is He that is in you, than he that is in the world.*

The "them" referred to is the false teachers – the antichrists who daily surround us. The "little children spoken to are us …, His children.

The message to us further states a very comforting truth of God; that He is greater than the ruler of this world, Satan. When we are faced with overwhelming evil forces we should, we must, remember God's promise to us contained in this memory Scripture. God, resting on the Sabbath is overwhelmingly stronger than the devil in his darkest and most evil night. This Scripture occurs in my mind more often than many others, and is a great God-given comfort.

1 John 4:20 – *If a man say, I love God, and hateth his brother, he is a liar; for he that loveth not his brother whom he hath seen, how can he love God whom he hath not seen?*

This memory verse is food for thought. The old deacon who stands in front of the flock claiming his unfaltering love for Jesus, but has animosity against his wife, business partner or the kid next door is a liar, according to God's truth displayed here. Taken literally here it appears if you hate someone – anybody, then your love for God is in question. Let's all learn to love our enemies and detest their sin.

1 John 5:7 – *For there are three that bear record in heaven, the Father, the Word, and the Holy Ghost: and these three are one.*

I believe this with all my heart …, but I don't understand it well enough to illuminate another's conception. I truly look forward to understanding it completely on the other side of Jordan, when we all will no longer see through a glass darkly.

2 John 1:9-11 – *Whosoever transgresseth, and abideth not in the doctrine of Christ, hath not God. He that abideth in the doctrine of Christ, he hath both the Father and the Son. 10 – If there come any unto you, and bring not this doctrine, receive him not into your house, neither bid him God speed: 11 – for he that biddeth him God speed is partaker of his evil deeds.*

Those polite, clean-cut young Mormons who park their bikes and ring your doorbell fit this description. Their religion teaches that Jesus Christ is not God, but a brother to Satan! That is hardly the doctrine of Christ. The nicely dressed Watchtower ladies miss the mark, also. We should politely send them away, based on this memory Scripture.

If you quietly quote it to them they usually shake their heads and leave. We all probably have enough evil deeds to repent of without partaking of theirs.

3 John 1:2 – *Beloved, I wish above all things that thou mayest prosper and be in health, even as thy soul prosperth.*

This is a salutation to a church leader named Gaius whom John is applauding as he hopes to re-visit that congregation soon. It shows John's good feelings for, and interest in the people there. John equated the importance of prosperity, physical health, and the condition of the soul.

Jude 1:21 – *Keep yourselves in the love of God, looking for the mercy of our Lord Jesus Christ unto eternal life.*

This short memory verse is taken from one of the shorter books of the Bible, only twenty-five verses long. It was written by Jude, a half-brother to Jesus about thirty years after Jesus was returned to sit at the right side of the Father. Jude is encouraging his fellow Christians of the importance of relying on God for our eternal lives in heaven. This is something of greatest importance today also.

Revelation 3:20 – *Behold, I stand at the door, and knock: if any man hear my voice, and open the door, I will come in to him, and sup with him, and he with me.*

This lovely memory verse is spoken in such warm expression as to show Christ as wanting to be a friend and intimate associate – a brother, and co-heir with us. We only need to hear His plea and invite Him into our home …, and into our heart.

Revelation 21:4 – *And God shall wipe away all tears from their eyes; and there shall be no more death, neither sorrow, nor crying, neither shall there be any more pain: for the former things are passed away.*

These promises from our Savior are, to me, among the very most tender and sweetest in the entire Bible. With no pain, crying, death, nor tears there it will be as – no, not as, but it will be heaven. And remember, this isn't for a season, as the lusts of the world are, this is FOREVER!!!

Revelation 22:16 – *I Jesus have sent mine angel to testify unto you these things in the churches. I am the root and the offspring of David, and the bright and morning star.*

This poetic memory verse reminds us of the accurate predictions of the prophets, that the Savior of men's souls would be of the house (descended from) King David. His blessed mother, Mary, was a descendent of David, hence Jesus also. Those prophets of old made many other predictions related to Jesus, and they were ALL spot on!

Revelation 22:17 – *And the Spirit and the bride say, come. And let him that heareth say, come. And let him that is athirst come. And whosoever will, let him take the water of life freely.*

Other passages in the Bible compare an unsaved person as someone who is thirsty. Next to air to breathe, our need for water is paramount. Someone without any food can live for a month or two; that person without water can only survive for a few days. Those living without the salvation offered freely by Jesus cannot live in heaven EVER. It is our responsibility, having been given the water of eternal life by Him, to bring His offer to other thirsty souls everywhere.

Revelation 22:18 -19 – *For I testify unto every man who heareth the words of the prophesy of this book. If any man shall add unto these things, God shall add unto him the plagues that are written in this book: 19 – And if any man shall take away from the words of the book of this prophesy, God shall take away his part out of the book of life, and out of the holy city, and from the things which are written in this book.*

Well educated men who should know better, re-write God's Holy Bible as if they don't believe this Scripture. If I read it correctly, we may miss a chance to discuss their rash actions on the other side Jordan.

Revelation 22:20-21 – *He which testifieth these things saith, Surely I come quickly. Amen. Even so, come, Lord Jesus. 21 – The grace of our Lord Jesus Christ be with you all. Amen.*

Jesus' last words recorded in the Bible are where He said here, "Surely I come quickly." Elsewhere, at 1 Corinthians 15:52 we are told He will appear in the twinkling of an eye. Someone said that's 1/300th of a second, anyway, it surely is quickly.

AFTERWORD

Thus we come to the end of this little book based on favorite Scriptures selected by Shirley and me. There are literally thousands more to select from. I suggest you might start with some we have listed here, and expand yours from these.

Print them directly from The Bible and carry them with you and practice reciting them to yourself, until you have each verse in your heart. Then practice with a trusted friend proofing you from the printed copy or from the Bible. This friend must have patience and a genuine interest in what you are doing.

If you have enjoyed and benefited from this book, recommend it to others. You might enjoy the other books by this same author. These are "Bits of Christian Wisdom," "Bits of Practical Wisdom," and "Three Cats Tales" a children's book, co-authored with the better half, Shirley.

As I approach my eighty-third birthday, and we near our sixty-second wedding anniversary, we look back on our hours of Scripture recitation as one of our most pleasant endeavors.

All royalty proceeds from these books accrue to our nonprofit entity, the Gilbertex Foundation, Inc. This foundation provides Bibles and Christian literature to churches, prisons, and others. It also provides financial support to several small Protestant churches in Mexico, as well as missionaries there and in Indonesia, Malawi, and West Africa. You may visit our website at gilbertexfoundation.org for more information.

Yours in His service,
Vernon Gilbert, August, 2015
Romans XV:33

Printed in the United States
By Bookmasters